I CHOPPED OFF MY TITS

COPYRIGHT 2019 AMANDA KATHERINE LOY
ALL RIGHTS RESERVED.

NO PART OF THIS BOOK MAY BE REPRODUCED,
SCANNED, OR DISTRIBUTED IN ANY PRINTED OR
ELECTRONIC FORM WITHOUT PERMISSION.
ISBN: 9781711706795

I CHOPPED OFF MY TITS:

AND IT'S THE BEST & HARDEST DECISION I'VE EVER HAD TO MAKE

By Amanda Katherine Loy

This book is dedicated

To my Grandma Anna
& to all of the womxn in my life who have moved so many mountains.

You're strong. You're brave.
And you inspire me to live my fuck yes life every single day.

CONTENTS

Foreword by Dana Donofree of Anaono Intimates

Intro	1
Who The Fuck Am I?	5
WTF Is The Point Of This Book?	10

PART ONE: MY STORY

The C Word	15
The Year of the Unapologetic Woman	20
BRCA What?	26
The Mess of It All	30
My Hard AF Decision	33
What It's Really Like to Get Your Tits Chopped Off	47
And So The Imposter Syndrome Sets In	59
My Story Isn't Over	70

PART TWO: FEAR

Facing Your Fears Head On	78
My Body Dysmorphia Will Come Back	85
My Sex Life Is Going To Go Down The Dumps	95

If I Break Down, They'll See Me As Weak	108
My Life Is Never Going To Go Back To Normal	117
I'm Going To Have Franken-tits	128
I'm Going to Die	136
My Dog Isn't Going To Recognize Me	145
I Will Never Be Able To Have Kids	156
I Will Regret My Decision	168
I'm Going To Be Dirt Broke	176

PART THREE: THE AFTERMATH

What Happens When It's All Over?	187
Don't Be A Worry Wart	192
I Won't Have Anything Left To Fight For	196
I'm Still Going To Get Cancer	205
What Are Other People Going To Think?	210
She's Doing So Much Better Than I Am	219
My Scars Mean I'm Broken	227

The End...For Now	237
Acknowledgments	243

FOREWORD

I never had a choice. Ok, actually, I had a "choice" but not really. My life changed forever the day before my 28th birthday, nearly 10 years ago, when I was diagnosed with breast cancer. I had no family history (at least not strong enough to cause any concern or reality that one day it could happen to me), a clear annual check-up at the gyno and a planned wedding in just 2 months. Then cancer happened. That tiny little lump I found in my breast in the shower just weeks before turned out to be something that was going to try its damnedest to kill me. An aggressive form of breast cancer, and if my doctor had told me to wait and keep an eye on it, I would be dead.

So when I say I had a choice to remove my breasts or not, I didn't really. The options for me were limited. I could take several paths to treatment — I chose the most aggressive and I am glad I did because it is a big part of why I am here today to write and support this book and story of Amanda living her Fuck Yes life.

I see a divide in the breast cancer community community: those who are able to choose and those who are not. We cannot stand for this kind of divide. The way I see it, we are only stronger together. I see a genetic mutation as a diagnosis — a sure-fire diagnosis that the likelihood to one day get a cancer diagnosis is REAL.

I wonder what my life would have looked like if I had had the choice. If someone came to me a year earlier and said, "You will have breast cancer in 12 short months, it will change your life forever and you will never ever be the same. You will never wake up in the morning and not think of the disease that rests quietly in your body. You will have relationship problems, friendship challenges, and body issues. But you have one choice to stop it."

You know what my answer would have been? "FUCK YES! Take my breasts!"

Everyone has a story — many different, yet the same. That long, dark tunnel? We all stand in it. Some lights are brighter than others. I have been to more funerals than I can count, I have stood by the bedside of my dying friends. I have been forever changed by the people I have met since my diagnosis.

In reading this book, I hope you find the courage and openness to talk about life, fear, love and hope. Amanda does, and by sharing how she has navigated this strange world, I know this book will give hope for what we all face in life. To be able to overcome and come out a better person on the other side — because when you face your life and your fears head on, you can live your best AF life ever!

Dana Donofree
Breast cancer patient since 2010
Founder & CEO of AnaOno

INTRO

Have you ever had to make a hard as fuck decision? One that you felt sick to your stomach about but you KNEW you had to make? If you can't relate to this then congratu-fucking-lations, you're a magical unicorn. If you can, and you're like 99.9% of the world's population, then you get it and you know it sucks.

I've had to make a buttload of hard AF decisions over the years. You know the ones...from which beanie baby you were going to put in the clear boxes, and which ones you were going to play with; which Spice Girl you were most like; which boy you were going to try to get to fall in love with you; the prom dress you should choose...If getting a degree in musical theatre and moving far away from your family was the best decision you could ever make or just a stupid idea that would leave you unemployable. How to even begin to choose who to put in your bridal party. To admitting you need help about your binge eating or finally sucking up your pride and deciding to start seeing a therapist for your anxiety instead of just keeping on trying to navigate it on your own.

Yup, those are a handful of some of my personal hell decision making experiences throughout my lifetime. And I'm only twenty eight years old — I can't imagine all of the crazy ass things I'm gonna look back on when I'm a ninety year old granny living it up in my old age. *In case we haven't met in real life, I'm basically already a baby grandma so I'm super prepared for being the most badass grandma dancing up a storm with her walker, just you wait.*

But the biggest and baddest hard AF decision I ever had to make was deciding to chop off my tits. And since you're a the brightest bulb in the bunch and bought this book*¹ you know exactly what my decision was. Yup. On December 3rd, 2018, at the age of twenty seven, I chopped off my tits. Literally, hacked them off with a chainsaw. It's true.

Okay, ya weirdo, settle down. I didn't *actually* chop them off myself. I know, the visual can't leave ya no matter how hard you try. Sorry in advance. If you didn't already get the memo that shit is going to get weird on this journey we're about to embark together, then HERE IT IS IN NEON LIGHTS. Seriously, can you imagine, though? You're reading this and are like, "What the actual fuck this crazy girl wrote a book??!?!" Well, you can calm down because obviously, I wrote a book, 'cause hey, you're reading it. But I promise you, I definitely didn't go all

---

¹ *did ya like my alliteration there? I'm a MF modern day Shakespeare, I tell ya.*

Chainsaw Massacre on my own boobs. That would be another book entirely and if that's what you came for, I'm sorry to disappoint.

I did, however, make the very difficult decision to get a prophylactic bilateral mastectomy - or in normal people speak: a preventative double mastectomy. What I so lovingly refer to as "chopping off my tits". Yeah, I know. Intense. And while you are probably reading this and are surprised as hell that someone my age would have any reason to do this, let me tell ya, my story is not unique. It's one I've heard time and time again in the mouths of other womxn my age who are *just like me*. Yet it's never fucking talked about. And I'll be damned if it stays that way.

So that's why I decided to write this book. To shed some light about what it's really like to go through a surgery like this at my age. Why I made this decision in the first place. All the fears and anxieties I had along the way, and how I navigated the other side.

If you're reading this and are in the club — *aka your life has been affected by breast cancer in any way* — welcome home. And if you're not, this is for you too. Because whether you're going through something hard AF right this moment, just coming out of it or about to be hit on the head with a major curveball ('cause whether we like it or not, life is messy like that), we all have shit we're facing and by the end of this, you are gonna feel a hell of a lot less alone. Plus, I'm known in my circle for dishing out some major truth bombs that lead to hella inspired action so get ready for the goods and get ready to get one step closer to living your fuck yes life. Are you ready? Let's go.

WHO THE FUCK AM I?

Hey! I'm Amanda. I've lived in Chicago for the last ten years, but I'm originally from the great white north. O Canada! I'm a giant goofball - I have a plethora of laughs that are all incredibly unattractive to listen to, but my friends tell me are hilarious and endearing. I got married to my husband with ring pops at City Hall. I have an unhealthy obsession with my dog. I use the word fuck a shit ton more than the average person. Oh, and I'm an actor, mindset and wellness coach, podcast host, speaker and now I guess this would qualify me as a writer too? Well fucking eh, I'll take it! Basically, I'm a slasher*[2] and I wouldn't have it any other way.

When I was a kid, I used to climb this tree with my locked diary and be up there for hours writing. Yeah, I was one of those kids with locked diaries. Do they even make those anymore? I recently found

---

[2] *Term I've so lovingly dubbed as my endless desire to do all the things and never choose one career path because they all make me happy. Not a serial killer, Jeanine! Someone has clearly been watching too many Criminal Minds episodes.*

one of them while cleaning out my old room at my family home in Toronto and wow, did I have some big dreams. I wanted to be a professional ballerina. *Didn't happen. Not even close. More on that later.* I wanted to change the world. *Finish reading the book before you judge me on the likelihood of that one.* And I wanted to write a book that helped other people understand things better. So to say this is a dream come true is not the slightest exaggeration. Did I expect to write a book about one of the scariest and most challenging times of my life? Hell no. Did I ever anticipate I'd be recounting in detail about the process of having my breasts physically removed from my body and the emotional and physical toll that had on me? My twenty three year old self is having a panic attack as we speak just thinking about the vulnerability of it all. But in the past few years, I've learned so much about myself, what it means to be human, the intricacies of how our bodies and brains are so deeply connected and, more than anything, how to navigate fear and overwhelm without it leading to yet another sob fest on the bathroom floor wondering how you've gotten here again. And I've learned all of these things because I desperately needed them. I knew deep down that life couldn't always be so fucking hard. That navigating traumatic and emotionally draining situations didn't need to end in massive panic attacks, lashing out at loved ones or a series of unhealthy addictions. But I had no fucking clue how to get to the other side.

It's been a messy ride to say the least, and I'm still figuring shit out day by day, as we all are, but I've learned so much along the way. Things that I *wish* someone I related to had written a book about so I hadn't felt so damn alone on my journey. I would be remiss to not pay that the fuck forward.

So now, the big question…You're probably wondering what makes me more qualified to write a book than Nancy from next door with the weird chihuahua that never stops barking. And the answer is: nothing. Your badass self could decide to start writing about something one day and BAM, a book falls out. *If it really is that easy for you, call me and tell me everything you know.* In all seriousness though, I'm no different than you. I mean, our privileges and inherent biases may be drastically different. I'm a cis gendered bisexual Caucasian female living in the United States. I'm married to a man, able bodied and, according to my taxes last year, categorized as upper middle class. Sound like you? Cool. Aspects you identify with? Sweet. Completely different than who you are? Badass. This book is written from that lense 'cause it's the only lense I've got.*3 Unless one day shit gets all Freaky Friday on me and I end up living like Obama for a few months, I'm stuck with what I know and my perspectives from that place. *Don't worry, I'll confirm that Michelle's arms are*

---

3 **I do my best to be incredibly cognizant of all of the human beings I do not inherently represent throughout this book, but the truth is, I'm probably gonna fuck up because I'm human. So go easy on me, okay?*

as amazing in reality as you want them to be. But until that magical day arrives, I'm left with what I know, who I am at this snapshot moment in time, and the life I've lived thus far.

I want to be crystal fucking clear. What I write in this book is not truth with a capital "t", as my husband Kev likes to put it. But it's *my* truth, paired with a shit ton of research and learning that we deep dive into so you can in turn discover, cry, hopefully laugh your ass off to, and take inspired action in your own life. I don't want to be *the* voice around this. I want to be *a* voice. To inspire you to start the conversation in your own life around the topics we're about to deep dive into. Hell, I want to know what you think. What you feel differently about. How you tick. Because what's the damn point of being a living breathing being that has the capacity for critical thought if we don't flex that muscle and learn from one another, am I right?

My point a billion light years ago about you and I not being so different? I definitely digressed. But at the heart of it, we're all living creatures who at the very base level are the same and have the same needs. We sleep, we eat, we poop, we have sex (well, most of us do) and we find ways to pass the time in a myriad of ways. If my self conscious seven year old self can dream about writing a book about helping other people understand things better and it actually came true, then holy shit balls can your big ass dreams come true too.

Dream big and embrace the mess that will allow them to unfold. Don't worry, your deep dive into all things my mess is coming up super fucking quick. So get ready.

WTF IS THE POINT OF THIS BOOK?

I'm so glad you asked, Linda. This is not a boring ass science book about breast cancer. This is not like the latest celebrity autobiography that's semi amusing but mostly like a *Maury**[4] tell all that's almost too much to handle at times. This is also not your typical self help book where there's all the warm and fuzzy stuff, but you don't actually get any tangible tools to make an impact on your life.

While my copious amount of introductory material may have fooled you**, this book has turned into something beyond my wildest dreams. The truth? My adult self never planned to write a book. Hell, I didn't even realize that's what I was doing until I was six thousand words in and realized there was no way in hell I could put my thoughts into a blog post or podcast episode of this magnitude.

---

[4] *If you don't know what Maury is, google that shit. Also, I'm officially old.
**what can I say, I'm a talkative motherfucker.

So yeah, this book was a complete and utter accident. It literally poured out of my fingertips because I fucking had to share this shit. Share my story. Share the things I've learned along the way. And give a voice to the things that are never spoken about. So get ready for something you've never read before. The nitty gritty tell all of the true events of what chopping off my tits was really like. A deep dive into all things fear — how it holds us back in life and how we can take inspired action around it so we can feel empowered and live our fuck yes, unapologetic lives. And how to navigate the other side of trauma — the worries, the anxieties and beyond— from my personal experiences coupled with my work as a mindset coach. Because despite what we'd like to believe, the reality is that the hard shit we face in life never *really* leave us.

A few things to note before you dive in. This book is not meant to just make you laugh, cry and finally feel MF seen to your deepest core. It is meant to give you actionable tools that you can start implementing in your life to experience wild transformation. 'Cause I know you're tired of staying stuck in the mess sistah. I was tired too. So giddy up and let's do the damn thing.

Important terms I use through the book and what they mean:

Womxn: I never write the word woman or womxn in this book. For me, the term womxn allows me to include anyone that identifies as a female. Not just the gender you were born with.

Tools in your toolbox: Throughout the book, I've shared with you some of the most valuable mindset tools that I work on with my clients. Having a full toolbox from a mindset standpoint, to me, means having positive coping mechanisms to arm you when you're navigating the mess. To survive any trauma or shit storm, you need a shitload of tools. And with this lessons in each chapter, you're going to finally have a full toolbox to take show up intentionally in your life.

Inspired action: You can read all of the self development books you want, follow all of the inspiring coaches you can find online who share their tools, but nothing changes in your life until you actually implement them for yourself. That's what inspired action is all about. And why I reference it over and over again in the book.

Ultimately, this is not your mama's personal development book. This is your how-to-navigate-the-shit-storm-we-call-life manual. Just like an Ikea table where you read the manual and slowly but surely put it together, peg to hole and so on and so forth until you have a complete whole shiny ass table. This book is the Ikea table manual to putting your life back together again after it's been crumbled into a million pieces or you've experienced a massive transition in your life. Or, better yet, how to not just survive but thrive through the mess in the first place. Because the mess? The unexpected traumas? Potholes we accidentally bump up against in our lives? They're inevitable and often, out of our control. What we can control? How we arm ourselves to face the mess head on and live our fuck yes lives amidst it all. Let's fucking go.

SECTION ONE:

MY STORY

THE C WORD

I always assumed that one day, I would get breast cancer. It felt like everywhere I looked, womxn above the age of forty five were getting diagnosed and treated, so I just...expected it to happen to me. That one day, I would find a lump and my doctor would tell me that I too had breast cancer. I was so sure I wrote this in my diary when I was eleven years old. *Don't worry, I had evolved from the locked diary by that point to a much more adult one with the words "Live. Laugh. Love." adorning the cover. I know that you had one of those too, don't deny it.* This fear ran rampant through my life until, one day, it became all too real.

But my story doesn't start with me. It starts with my dad. The man that has taught me everything I know about patience, communication and adventuring. The person who dedicated years of his life to countless under-doggy pushes on our wooden swing in the backyard, soccer drills and laughs with our neighbourhood soccer team The Grasshoppers, and bedtime readings of *The Hobbit*. The man who when I told him I wanted to go to theatre school said: "Go for it. How can I support you?" My dad, who lost his mom to breast cancer when he was eighteen years old.

I remember hearing about my Grandma Anna when I was little and always wondering why I had never gotten to meet her. As soon as I was old enough to understand, my dad told me all about her and how she had died. I remember immediately feeling this unshakeable connection to her. And that connection never wavered.

Growing up, I found myself talking to her and asking her questions, even when I knew she wouldn't be able to respond. I would go visit her gravestone every time we went and stayed at my dad's family home away from home in a tiny town in the middle of nowhere Ontario, Canada. Every time I'd visit her, I would bring little gifts with me — a flower, a rock — anything to leave a reminder on her tombstone that I was there. And I'd sit there for hours. Crying. Asking her questions. Telling her how much I wished I had been able to meet her. And wondering what we would have talked about and done together had she still been alive.

Everyone that knew her and then met me always told me how much I was just like her. My laugh. My smile. My zest for life. My deep empathy for others. Hearing these things made me feel closer to her, yet incredibly sad at the same time. Even though I had never met her, I *knew* that she and I were kindred spirits and that we would have been the best of friends if she had still been alive. Call it whatever you want, but I had this inner knowing that there was a connection greater than our characteristics and being blood that bonded us. What I didn't realize at the time was how much she and I truly had in common.

Like so many womxn these days, my grandma was one of the many that had breast cancer. She was diagnosed when she was forty- two years old and two years later, she passed away. It was aggressive. It didn't play around. And it left my dad and his two younger sisters devastated. Losing a parent that young? I can't even begin to imagine it. I'm so grateful that I've never had to. But it certainly changed the trajectory of my dad's life, and as a result, it changed mine too.

Breast cancer is a bitch. Let's just put it out there for the world, ok? (In case ya haven't figured it out yet, I don't sugar coat things.) And this MF disease? It's awful. The past year alone, I've met so many incredible womxn *my age* getting diagnosed with breast cancer and it blows my mind every damn time. And while there is so much more work to do, thankfully, there have been a shit ton of advancements in research and treatment. And that's where *my story begins.*

When I was a kid, unbeknownst to me at the time, my dad got tested for the BRCA gene (pronounced "BRACA"). Information about this gene was just starting to become known in the medical world in Canada, and our family doctor urged my dad to get tested for it given his family history. You see, two genes had been discovered that, when mutated, were significantly linked to breast cancer, and a simple blood test could tell you if you had one of the mutations or not.

Now you're probably thinking … uh, but your dad is a dude. So why would it matter for him? We're talking about *breast* cancer here. Well, for one, men can get breast cancer. Yup, it's not common but super possible. Not to mention, any man with one of the BRCA mutations see an increased likelihood of developing prostate cancer in their lifetime. And most importantly to him, the BRCA gene mutation has a 50/50 chance of being genetically passed down to any offspring. In other words, if he had the mutation, there was a huge chance I was royally screwed.

So, he took the test alongside my two aunts. Thankfully, they both were negative for the gene but my dad wasn't so lucky. When I was in high school, he sat me down and told me that he had tested positive for the BRCA 1 gene, and my naive little heart didn't think twice about it. I was young. I was healthy. And I didn't need to think about something like that for years…or so I thought. All of the encouragement in the world couldn't have convinced my seventeen year old self to get tested, and so I moved to Chicago to pursue my dream of being an actor and didn't think about it again.

Or so my family thought. In truth? It ate me alive. I thought about it all of the time, I just didn't talk about it. My journal was the only place that knew my fears inside and out. The first time I let someone in about my fears on the matter was on my very first date with Kevan, the man I'm so goddamn lucky to be married to. I didn't know him outside of that guy in my forensic sciences class in the red shirt that seemed a little cocky, but after some serious convincing on his part, I finally agreed to go out with him. Our first date was like something you would see in the movies — I hate myself for writing that but it's true. It felt like I had known him for years. We laughed. We got into intense philosophical debates. We shared deeply personal details about our lives. So much so that I felt comfortable sharing the words "getting breast cancer" in response to his question "what's your greatest fear?". That's not the only thing I revealed on our first date either… we got weird (what else is new) and ended up laughing about buying the other diapers in our old age. Yup, it was goofy and amazing and all of the things in between…but that's for another story.

My point is that the fear of getting breast cancer? It was deeply rooted inside of me for years. And, deep down, I knew that it was only a matter of time before it got me too. But I still held out a small glimmer of hope that I would be the lucky one. And the fear of knowing my "fate" and getting tested for the gene made it feel real, and I just couldn't gather up the strength to know. So I didn't…Until I did.

THE YEAR OF THE UNAPOLOGETIC WOMAN

I stopped making New Year's resolutions and bucket lists years ago. They felt contrived, you know? I mean, there were only so many years running a 5k could be on the list without me genuinely admitting to myself that no, I did not want to run a 5k. I didn't want to run, period. *Okay, if you love running, you get all the gold stars in the world and I truly am in awe of you, but it's not and never will be for me.*

When I started my business in the fall of 2015, I deep dove into the personal development world like a kid in a candy store. I had never touched a book like that in my life, unless you count my teenage romantic self crying while reading *Eat Pray Love* and dreaming about what life in Bali and meeting my soulmate would look like. Can you guess what else was on my bucket list? Who am I kidding, take me to Bali.

But the thought of stepping into the "self help" section of the bookstore? I thought I was *way above* all of that. I didn't need the help. Those books were for people with issues. Or so I kept telling myself. Until I opened up my first book and dove into the self development world head first and never looked back. And now, I'm writing this self development meets real talk meets true life autobiography goodness so, clearly I've drank the koolaid. And I hope you have too, 'cause when you truly pour into this world and take action on the things you learn, the potential for transformation is in-fucking-credible.

The first thing I did when I started my journey? Got MF clear on what I actually cared about and who I truly was. I had spent so much of my life trying to be this perfect version of myself. Transform into what everyone else wanted and needed from me that I had spent so little time actually getting to know myself and figure out what *I wanted*, what *I needed* and how *I wanted to feel*. And part of that discovery has been a new yearly ritual to replace my NY resolutions — my word of the year. Every year, in December, I take some time to really take stock of my year.

I carve out a day in my calendar to be just for me and I sit with my journal and ask questions to myself like...

What are you most proud of this year?
When did you feel most alive?
What did you have to overcome?
What is missing in your life?
What energy are you craving more of in the coming year?

And I take note of what words I'm using. And every time, I find myself seeing the same word pop up over and over again...and heading into 2018, the word unapologetic was hitting me in the face over and over again. It felt right. I was craving a big upleveling in my business. I was tired of dimming my light and playing small to make other people feel more comfortable. And the word unapologetic? It felt like freedom.

My unapologetic self?

She stopped apologizing for being "too much" or "too bold".
She faced her fears head on.
She swore, all the fucking time.
She took risks.
She advocated for herself and knew her worth.
She said YES when it felt right and NO when it didn't.
She was fully herself.

I knew I needed to embody that version of me, but I was scared shitless to do so. I had lived so much of my life on automatic pilot, dimming parts of me to fit in. How was the world going to see me? Would my friends and family still accept me? Would my business fail? Would I have the strength to face my fears head on? I didn't know the answers, but I knew it was time to take the leap and find out.

And it all started with finally facing my biggest fear and getting tested for the BRCA gene. So I went to my doctor, requested the blood test and two weeks later, in the middle of January, I got my blood drawn and sent off to get tested. You'd think the next couple of weeks waiting to find out the answers would be pure torture. And in some ways, it was. I don't do well with things being out of control -- you know? But, to be honest, every fibre of my being knew I was positive. It felt like I was just waiting for the confirmation so I could officially make some HARD AF decisions and move on with my life. What I wasn't prepared for was my reaction when I found out.

Two days after my 27th birthday, I got the call. I was feeling so good that day. I had written all about what I was going to accomplish that year and I could see it all happening so clearly. I was confident. Standing in my truth for the first time in my life and I felt like nothing could bring me down. *A feeling I had desired so deeply for years.* And then, in a matter of minutes, it all came crashing down.

Have you ever gotten a phone call that changed the entire trajectory of your life? Having my doctor call me that day and mutter the words: "your test results came back and you are positive for the BRCA 1 gene" felt like that for me. The rest of the day was a blur but what I remember was this: I hung up the phone and sat there, stunned. I called Kev and quickly told him. Then called my parents and told them. And as soon as I hung up, I started to sob uncontrollably. I ripped off my clothes and ran to my bathroom, turned on the shower and spent the next 45 minutes crying. That last bit of hope? The tiny sliver of light I had that I could possibly be negative was officially lost. And I knew that my world was about to change in ways I couldn't possibly begin to imagine, and that scared the living daylights out of me.

So yeah, that full fledged shower breakdown you see in movies? I was that girl. And that's exactly how Kev found me after he rushed home from work. Naked. Completely drenched. Eyes puffy and red from crying and completely dazed. I know you know the one.

I was such a mixed bag of emotions. I didn't know what to do with myself. I was scared. So scared. Sad. Angry. And I was also incredibly relieved. Relieved I finally had an answer. Relieved I had the privilege to *make a choice*. And so damn determined to be an advocate for womxn just like me who spent hours googling information about being in your twenties and dealing with this and came up with nothing. Who joined BRCA support groups on Facebook only to find themselves surrounded by fifty year old plus womxn who were sharing the most graphic photos of their post mastectomy bodies that made you wanna die a little inside. Don't get me wrong — I'm grateful for their vulnerability and willingness to be so open about their journeys. But I just couldn't relate to them. I wasn't 55. I hadn't already had kids. And I certainly was nowhere close to the brink of menopause. And I felt so fucking alone.

My family and friends were incredibly supportive but they didn't get it. How could they? Once you find out you have BRCA, it's like you join a secret club. And all of a sudden, a huge part of your life becomes something that everyone you love can't relate to. So you look elsewhere, but what happens if that search comes up blank? It's a billion times more terrifying, right? Well, that's exactly what happened for me when I first found out I was BRCA positive. And after I came up for air from my breakdown, I knew that this was my opportunity to make sure nobody ever felt alone on their journey again.

Maybe you're nodding your head and resonate with this journey on a cellular level. Or maybe you've never had to deal with BRCA or breast cancer but have been through some traumatic shit in your life. That feeling of loneliness and utter despair and overwhelm? It can feel like nobody will ever begin to understand what we're going through, and maybe some of them won't, but I hope just by reading this you can begin to see that you are so not alone. You have the power to move mountains and fully step into your power.

It isn't easy, but it's so goddamn worth it.

BRCA WHAT?

I would be remiss to not write a chapter solely dedicated to what BRCA actually is, because let's face it, while this book is about so much more than BRCA and fighting against breast cancer (*yay trauma and hard AF shit -- if that's not part of your human experience, you may want to make sure that you're not half robot*), that piece of my journey was the impetus for writing this book in the first place. So what the actual fuck is BRCA anyways? Here are the MF facts.

What is BRCA anyways?

BRCA 1 and BRCA 2 are human genes that produce tumor suppressor proteins. We all have these in our bodies -- hooray! However, when either of these genes are mutated, cells in the body are more likely to develop additional genetic alterations that can lead to cancer. Inheriting the BRCA1 or BRCA2 gene increases the risk of female breast and ovarian cancers (although they have also been associated with several additional types of cancer). People who have inherited mutations in

BRCA1 and BRCA2 tend to develop breast and ovarian cancers at younger ages than people who do not have these mutations.

How do you inherit the mutation?

A BRCA1 or BRCA2 mutation can be inherited from someone's mother or father. Each child of a parent who carries a mutation in one of these genes has a 50% chance (or 1 chance in 2) of inheriting the mutation. As I mentioned earlier, when I was young, my dad got tested and found out that he had the BRCA 1 gene. Most womxn my age that I've spoken to who know about the gene were urged to get tested after their moms or close female relatives were diagnosed with breast or ovarian cancer. Of the hundreds of womxn I've met with BRCA, I've only met one other gal who has a similar story to mine and found out through her father. So if you have any history of breast or ovarian cancer on either side of your family, you may want to consider getting tested.

What are the numbers though? Like the cold hard facts?
For BRCA 1[*5]:

- 60-80% risk of developing breast cancer over lifetime compared to the 12% general population risk.

---

[5] *stats pulled from the National Society of Genetic Counselors*

- 34-44% risk of developing ovarian cancer over lifetime compared to the 1-2% general population risk.
- 2-3 % risk of developing pancreatic cancer over lifetime compared to the 0.9% general population risk.
- Increased risk in male breast and prostate cancer

For BRCA 2:

- 50-70% risk of developing breast cancer over lifetime compared to the 12% general population risk.
- 12-20% risk of developing ovarian cancer over lifetime compared to the 1-2% general population risk.
- 20-30% risk of developing prostate cancer over lifetime compared to the 16% general population
- 7% risk of developing male breast cancer over lifetime compared to the 1.10% general population
- 3-5 % risk of developing pancreatic cancer over lifetime compared to the 0.9% general population risk.
- 3-5 % risk of developing melanoma over lifetime compared to the 1-2% general population risk.

Okay...so should I consider genetic testing?

- You have a relative with a BRCA 1 or BRCA 2 mutation

- You have family history of breast cancer diagnosis at an early age (aka before 50 years of age)
- You have a family history of ovarian cancer
- There are multiple generations in your family with breast and/or ovarian cancer
- A family member has had multiple primary cancers
- You have any Ashkenazi Jewish ancestry (this one took me by surprise! I have Ashkenazi Jewish ancestry on both sides of my family and didn't realize it played a role in this particular mutation)

I know facts are sometimes boring. This theatre obsessed creative gal who hated math class feels that on a level you can only imagine. But knowledge is power. Especially when it comes to our health. And I'm all about advocating the fuck out of that and that meant putting the nitty gritty super terrifying numbers out there for ya. If they scared you as much as they did me when I first saw them, I'm here with you sistah. And you may be hating me right now*[6] and feeling all sorts of fear and anxiety and I'm here to tell you that that's okay. And that's why you're here. I've got you. Keep reading and stick with me. We're in this together and I promise, if I can get through this, you can too.

---

[6] *really great Amanda. Already alienating the reader with your real AF ways. Who am I kidding? I know you appreciate this shiz, even if it's hard. Because you're a MF warrior and you can do hard things.

THE MESS OF IT ALL

If there's one thing you need to know about me it's that I lay it all out on the table, always. I'm honest to a fault. And I believe that sharing the mess is the only way to be honest. Throughout my journey, I journaled a lot. And while going back through past entries, I found my first real brain dump let out all the feelings around my journey with BRCA a week after the doctor called me. I was in Hawaii with my best friend Rina and for the first time amidst our bonding time together and adventuring, I decided to take some time to myself and sit on the beach and journal…

The second I got back from the gym to an empty room and found myself truly alone for the first time in a week? It all came rushing in. I am a woman living with the BRCA 1 gene. I have a 72% chance of getting breast cancer before I'm 80 and a 44% chance of getting ovarian cancer. That is fucking terrifying.

And in all of this, the biggest thing that continues to ring true in my brain is this is the reason I decided to get tested in the first place — to quit the fear cycle and know once and for all.

So the "option" of screening doesn't feel like an option to me because FUCK just cancer to come. I mean, I'd kick it in the ass but goddamn if I take that chance.

The things I know?

I'm terrified.

I don't know what this means for my future as a mom. My identity. My self worth. My strength. My marriage. Everything feels unknown.

Everything feels foreign and completely different than it did. All of my plans and dreams feel...hard to imagine now. (Which I know is so silly but it's my reality right now so I'm leaning in and trying to accept my emotions).

I know that I will be chopping my boobs off, stat. Fuck.

I've been intuitively preparing my life for this. My health? There's a reason I took control of it when I did. The platform I have built? This is everything. This may be a story I never imagined for my life but it's mine and goddamnit, I intend on bringing light to this and being a light for others.

This is going to be a huge year of change. I don't quite know what that means but I know that no matter what it looks like, I am strong and I am supported.

I can and I will navigate this. With strength. And all the mess in between.

Because it's my mess.

You've got this girl.

I share this with you because it's the exact snapshot of what truly being in the mess was like for me. Because I know you're in it too, sister. This world? It's messy. And we are endlessly facing challenging things that really make us question if we're capable of navigating it all. The best thing I have learned on my journey? Embrace the mess. It's part of the journey to getting to the other side.

MY HARD AF DECISION

To be honest, the actual decision to chop off my tits was easy. I knew before I was BRCA positive that if I was, I was going to go through with the surgery. My doctors urged me to go the surveillance route and not make any hasty decisions, but I knew that surgery was the only option for me. I had spent the last 10 years waiting around for breast cancer, and goddamnit I wasn't going to spend any more of my life worrying about the day I found a lump.

That being said, the ten month journey between finding out I had the gene mutation to having the surgery was the most challenging, invigorating, overwhelming and anxiety inducing time of my life. As I'm sure you've experienced in your own life, just because you know what decision you need to make doesn't make it an *easy* one. When I told my friends and family that I was going through with the surgery, everyone in my life looked at me and saw a brave woman. I, on the other hand? I saw a woman scared shitless, coming apart at the MF seems, making the only decision she knew how to make. Don't get me wrong, it wasn't all bad. Despite my best efforts, I still have some deeply ingrained drama queen tendencies left over from childhood.*7 There were certainly some days when I felt on top of the world. Grateful I had the ability to make a decision, and ready to close this chapter so I could move on with my life. But other days, most days, I found myself curling up in the fetal position, riddled with fear and freaking out about how this was going to change my life. A life that I had worked so hard for. That it was going to change *me*. A person I had finally actually started to *like* and be *proud of*. I'd spent years undoing habits that didn't serve me and moving away from.

And this? It felt like a total wrench in my trajectory. And goddamnit, I liked the trajectory I was on. I was finally feeling confident in my own skin. I hadn't had a binge eating episode in over a year. I looked in the mirror and didn't pick *everything* about myself apart anymore. My marriage was in such a beautiful, playful and deeply supportive place. And I truly felt like I was living out my purpose in life with my business and my life as an actor.

How was this surgery going to impact all of those things? Would my business fail because I had to take a month off to recover? How would I feel about my body after surgery? Would I be comfortable having sex? How would that impact my marriage? Would my body dysmorphia come back? Was everyone going to look at me like a charity

---

7 *If only we could turn back time so you could see my one woman rendition of the entire production of Cats the musical that went down in my childhood home. It was pretty fucking epic.

case? I know, I know, irrational AF but nevertheless, legitimate FEARS I had about it all. Hell, I read an article about how after major surgeries, your body composition shifts and so your scent can change and it can cause your animals to not recognize you...which was basically my worst nightmare because my dog Toby is the love of my life. Don't worry, Kev is well aware and on the same page.*[8] It may sound ridiculous, but to me, it was just one of a buttload of what ifs going on in my mind. It's safe to say, the anxiety was *real* and the overwhelm set in hard.

After weeks of feeling my feels, going down the google spiral of hell, journaling and talking for hours about all of this with Kev, my family and my best friends, I finally asked myself a question that changed the game for me and it was this:

Are you going to let this experience define you, or are you going to define this experience?

The most important lesson I've learned in my self development journey is that **we can either let life happen to us, or allow it to happen for us**. The one thing we always have a say over are our thoughts and reactions to any situation. You can roll your eyes all you want (I know I spent years being like yeah yeah yeah that's some bullshit), but as someone who's lived on both sides, I promise you, it's true.

---

[8] *As soon as we started letting Toby sleep on the bed cuddled up in between us, there was just no looking back.

Case and point: After gaining 30 lbs in a year and developing a serious binge eating disorder, I perpetuated those habits for years and stayed unhappy and unhealthy. It was so hard to see any good in my situation and I let it lead my life for years. I lived out the belief that food was going to control my life forever. Until one day, I was sitting in my car, having just inhaled an entire sleeve of oreos in five minutes, and I started to bawl my eyes out — which, unfortunately, was pretty par for the course at that time in my life. But this time, a flip switched inside of me and I screamed at the top of my lungs in my 2003 Toyota Corolla, "If it's the last thing I do, I'm going to be healthy & happy and binge free".

That was my rock bottom. The day I decided that enough was enough.

It didn't happen overnight but slowly but surely, I made positive steps towards healing and I'm sitting here, so amazed that I can say that I am two years binge free, and I get to spend every day helping other womxn just like me recover from their binge eating and emotional eating tendencies too. All because I *decided* to change my story.

It's hard to see the light at the end of the tunnel when we're knee deep in the shit of it all. So hard that we can spend years on automatic pilot, perpetuating these beliefs that we aren't capable of changing our story. But you are. And you don't have to hit rock bottom to shift your perspective and start a new chapter — you can do it right fucking now with *anything* you're navigating in your life.

Think I'm a unicorn? I promise you I'm far from it, although I have created a life for myself that's pretty fucking magical. The truth is I'm a normal girl who spent too many years feeling miserable, overwhelmed, unhealthy, burnt out and unhappy and I decided to MF do something about it.

And you can too. No matter what you're navigating right now — if it's finding out you have the BRCA mutation, got diagnosed with cancer or a chronic illness, a breakup, a BS job thang or maybe you just spent the past hour in traffic and it pissed you the fuck off -- here's a tool that will change the game for all of the messy and frustrating parts of your life:

The FUCK It Method

I use a method I have so lovingly dubbed the FUCK it method, and you can too.

Here's the 411 breakdown:

1. **F**eel your feels, for a little bit
2. **U**plevel your mindset and take control
3. **C**hoose a desired feeling
4. **K**ick into action and move towards that feeling instead of away from it

See how I made that super fucking easy to remember? 'Cause trauma is HARD AF and I know you don't have time for that shit so literally all you have to remember is FUCK. Which I *know* you can do, you magical goddess.

And in using it, it's gonna look different for all of us, because we are all different human beings. So use this in the way that feels the most impactful for you. That being said, if you're a sucker for examples and are like "Amanda, how do you even begin to implement this shiz?"— I've got you.

Here's how the FUCK it method went for me when I found out I had the BRCA 1 gene:

Feel your feels, for a little bit

Truthfully, I failed at my own method for the first 2 weeks after I found out — proof that this journey we call life is far from perfect and cookie cutter. I hid from feeling anything. And it kinda happened by accident because the day after I found out, I flew to California for a business conference and then spent the next two weeks driving up the coast to San Francisco with the hubs and then finally ended up in Hawaii with my best friend for a girls trip.

I had moments of feeling my feels before I got to Hawaii (between my shower breakdown the day of and a follow up sob fest in the car on the way from LA to San Francisco where Kev calmed me down by making me laugh about my future teleportation tits — more on that later), but the first two weeks post phone call, my plate was so full up with all the things that I didn't have time to emotionally process anything. Hello, unintentional numbing! I should win a gold metal for that shit, I excel at it.

It wasn't until day five on my week long Hawaii adventure, when I took an afternoon to myself, that I found myself sitting on the beach, staring into the ocean and giving myself the space to finally feel it all. And the bawling my eyes out process began. This looked a lot like crying. Journaling. Yelling into pillows. The deluge of "why me" and feeling sorry for myself, and binge watching all of the romantic comedy movies I knew would make me cry. My girl Adele was on repeat. The best advice I can give you when it comes to anything hard AF in your life? Allow yourself to feel it.

Uplevel your mindset and take control

The thing about feeling your feels? It can be super easy to wallow in your emotions. And before you know it, you've watched eight seasons of *How I Met Your Mother* on Netflix (that "Are you still watching" pop-up message has come up more times than you care to admit) and you haven't gotten off of your couch in more days than you can count.

If you're there, it's OK. I feel you. But sister, it's time to shift into step U of the FUCK it method and uplevel outside of the feels and take some control of your life.

Does that mean you're going to magically stop feeling sad / angry / frustrated / hurt / confused etc. Hell no. But there are only so many pints of Ben & Jerry's you can eat before you realize the only thing that can make you feel better is YOU.

Upleveling our mindset? It takes a simple SHIFT in focus. Instead of focusing on everything that was going wrong and all my fears and anxieties about the situation, I shifted my focus to what I was grateful for. I looked for the positives in a royally shitty situation, and I asked myself: what do I have control over? For me? It looked a lot like: My reactions. Setting myself up with the surgical team that supported me and my needs. Surrounding myself with positive humans that will support me through this. Moving my body every day and working on building my strength with my workouts. Fueling my body with healthy, nutrient dense foods. How I spend my time. Connecting with other womxn who were also BRCA positive and understand what I was going through. Getting a therapist.

What's on your list? No, for real. Put the book down and take out your journal or phone and jot that shit down. *In case ya didn't get the memo, inspired action is my thing. 'Cause you can read all the things but if you aren't taking action then what's the fucking point, am I right? You know I'm not the type to sugar coat things...*

There is a shit ton that's outside of our control every single day, but there's also a shit ton of shit that is. Focusing on the latter is what gives us agency in our own lives. And I don't know about you, but waiting around like a sitting duck and letting life happen to me is not how I want to live my life.

Choose a desired feeling.

I knew that throughout my surgery and recovery process I wanted to feel STRONG, EMPOWERED and SUPPORTED. So my entire time leading up to surgery, I printed those words out around my house and looked at them every damn day. On days when I felt that way and on days when I felt FAR from strong, empowered and supported, they were beautiful reminders of how I wanted to show up intentionally.

Kick into action and move towards that feeling

It's one thing to state how you *want* to feel, and it's a whole other to take action so that you can actually feel that way. So as soon as I identified how I wanted to feel, I created an action plan:

Strong

To me, feeling strong was two-fold. I knew that in order to have a smooth recovery, being at my physically fittest was important. Plus, did you know that moving your body 30 minutes a day significantly decreases your risk of getting cancer? *Of course you did because you read shit and are smart AF.* Not to mention a shitload of other diseases. Le duh. Thankfully, I run fitness accountability groups every month so I had the resources at my fingertips to dive in. And that's exactly what I did the seven months leading up to my surgery.

Feeling strong to me also meant having positive coping mechanisms for my anxiety. 'Cause let me tell ya, there were days when it felt out of fucking control. My workouts were a huge piece of this too. Those endorphins? Elle Woods wasn't lying. And I started seeing a therapist every week for the first time in my life. Best. Decision. Ever.

Empowered

The way I saw it, I had two choices. I could let myself feel down in the dumps about "having to have this surgery" and go all woe is me, "why is this happening to me". OR, I could flip my motha-fucking perspective and view this as empowering as hell. 'Cause the reality is, this surgery for me? It was 100% a choice. I could have taken the surveillance route. Waited. Hoped I never got cancer. But I didn't want to go that route. I had the opportunity to do something to eliminate the risk. And that choice? It's truly a gift, and one that I am endlessly grateful for.

The other thing I took action on that was terrifying as all hell but ended up being more empowering than I could have imagined? Sharing my story in real time. Now I'll be the first to say that this is *not* for everyone. I have been sharing my story and my heart in the public eye for almost five years now, so I was hella used to getting vulnerable with my peeps. That being said, I'd never done it in real time before. I had always shared my story online after I had overcome what I was struggling with. But this time? I shared knee deep in the trenches, and the amount of womxn that came out of the woodworks messaging me about their journey and sharing their "me too" stories with me was astounding. Knowing that I wasn't alone and that by simply sharing my journey, I could maybe help change *one* person's life? That was the most empowering thing to me and ended up being a huge piece of the action I took moving into my BRCA journey as a result.

Supported

We're not all blessed with an incredible support system. While I am super lucky on that front family wise, I've also worked my butt off the few years leading up to my surgery creating a network of support. That being said, there were many moments leading up to my surgery and after the fact where I felt utterly alone. So my best advice? Start from within. Ask yourself how you can serve and support your own heart before you look to others. Schedule self care dates in your calendar. Say no to things you genuinely don't want to do and yes to the things that light your soul on fire.

As for outward support, the two best things I did were:
- **Ask for it.** I struggle a lot with trying to do everything myself. I'm independent AF and the idea of someone having to wait on me hand and foot or be there for me feels ridiculous. But going through something like this alone was something I knew I wouldn't be able to handle. So I asked for help. My mom came down for 2 weeks during my surgery. My husband took 3 weeks off work to be home, bathe me, look after our dog, cook and basically be my saving grace. And my friends and family? I told them it would make me SO happy to receive letters and care packages while I was recovering and they showed up like crazy.

Don't have a partner/supportive family? I bet you have one person in your life that would drop everything and be there for you. But they won't know that's what you need unless you ask for it.

- **Find a community with people that get it.** Getting connected and becoming actively involved with a local chapter of womxn navigating what I was going through was huge for my journey. These womxn? They understood. They were either in the trenches with me or had already been through it and their support has been unparalleled. Don't know where to start when it comes to finding people who understand what you're going through? Online groups, social media or even local meetups are constantly going on. Hell, I created the Live Your F*ck Yes Life membership so that support could go beyond just community but deep dive into actionable mindset tools, access to guest experts and beyond 'cause nothing like that existed. Do your research, commit to something that you know will support your needs, create something, and/or spend some time connecting with people who make you feel less alone.

And so the FUCK it method reigns on. This is the number one tool I share inside of my membership and with all of my clients, and is something I personally use all the time while going through something challenging in my life (which let's be honest, happens on the regular). So the next time something happens and you're on the precipice of a breakdown, and if you're anything like me you scream the word FUCK, lean into that word in a new and empowering way and walk yourself through the steps. You're more powerful than you know. Take agency of your life. And let that warrior I see inside of you emerge.

WHAT IT'S REALLY LIKE TO GET YOUR TITS CHOPPED OFF

The truth of the matter is no matter how much your controlled freak self prepares for something like this, it's always going to go differently than you've planned. That's life - am I right? We have all these expectations on how something is going to go, read up on it for hours so we can be ready to handle whatever comes and then BAM, we get totally blindsided by how things actually go. I had built up this surgery in my head as the hardest thing I was ever going to have physically faced. And while I'd argue that it was one of the most challenging things I have ever had to navigate emotionally, physically, I was shocked at how seamless the entire process ended up being for me.

Now, for all you gals out there considering this surgery/or rocking your previvor status already (and even if that's not you, listen up 'cause this shiz is important), I'm about to get a little Hermione Granger on ya so you can fully understand what I personally went through. Yup, as you'd imagine, this surgery can vary in a shit ton of ways for different people depending on a number of factors. My unique surgery was a

DTI, OTM bilateral nipple sparing prophylactic mastectomy procedure.

What the fuck does that mean? Here's some lingo to breakdown to help ya out:

DTI = Direct to implant. I was lucky to be a candidate for a one step procedure for a few reasons, according to my plastic surgeon — 1. I'm young, healthy and fit & 2. I wasn't looking to go up a cup size. Often, during the initial surgery to remove the breast tissue, something called expanders*[9] are inserted in place of implants for a few months leading up to a separate exchange surgery when the implants get inserted. More womxn go this route than not, for a myriad of reasons so if you're gearing up for a double mastectomy yourself, know that that could very well be the best path for you!

OTM = Over the muscle. This is in reference to where the implant is placed. It can either go over the muscle, or under the muscle. When placing the implant under the muscle, the surgery involves more initial trauma to your pectoral muscles and, as a result, can often lead to a longer physical recovery. From my experience, most surgeons advocate for under the muscle because cosmetically speaking, you're going to get a more realistic end result. Over the muscle is a pretty new way of doing

---

[9] *a temporary device that is shaped just like an implant and is designed to stretch the skin and muscle to make room for a future, more permanent implant. Sexy, I know. Basically, what I'm saying is we're all robots.

I CHOPPED OFF MY TITS

things and, because of that, my surgeon was definitely more comfortable with under the muscle, but after speaking to my surgeons and my fellow previvors, I knew that OTM was the right decision for me so I MF advocated for myself and am SO happy that I did -- wavy tits and all!

Bilateral prophylactic mastectomy — double preventative (aka I did/do not have cancer) removal of both breasts.

Nipple sparing — I opted to keep my nipples, many womxn don't.*[10]

Anyways, back to the surgery itself. The idea of it scared the living SHIT out of me. I had only ever had one major surgery in my life and it was when I was 19 years old and I had my tonsils removed, but that was something I wanted to do. When you have strep throat for six months in a row (the amount of puss coming out of me could have filled an entire hot air balloon**), and your doctor says getting your tonsils removed will significantly reduce your likelihood of having chronic strep, you get them the fuck out.

This? This was something I would have never made the decision to do without a good ass reason. I mean, don't get me wrong, I was never obsessed with my boobs. They were always farther apart than

---

[10] *This can be a personal choice or depending on the patient, one that needs to happen based on their specific circumstances. As always, consult your doctor before deciding to go rogue and SAVE THE NIPS if you can't!
** Ewwww, David. I know, I'm gross AND I love Schitts Creek.

I'd have wanted and shaped a bit like pears*11, but I had never for a second considered getting implants. So many people would say things like "well, silver lining, you get amazing boobs! It's like a free boob job!" — which, for the record, never say that to someone going through a surgery like this. It's nothing like a boob job, it pisses us off, and more importantly, it's not a MF bonus because in an ideal world, we genuinely don't want to have to go through a surgery like this. Hell, I seriously considered going flat for a while but didn't think that would translate well as a 20 something year old who spends a lot of her time performing on stage as an actor.

My point light years later is that major surgery was a pretty foreign concept to me, and I imagine it is for you as well. Or maybe you're scared AF leading up to getting a mastectomy yourself and you're reading this book as a what the fuck do I do guide? Or maybe, you're on the other side like me and just so goddamn thrilled a book was written about the ins and outs of this shit and everything we face. *My rage about there being little to no resources for womxn my age navigating this was THE VERY*

---

11 *The fact that we think we're less worthy or beautiful or sexy because our boobs are weird is something this entire process has made me hyper aware of. I've seen a BUNCH of boobs in the past year. More than I ever thought I'd see in my lifetime and, as a bisexual woman, I'm attracted to womxn! And let me tell ya, even cosmetically shifted ones look hella different. So MF embrace the boobs you've got sistah. If not for you, do it for me and all the BRCA babes out there. I know I'm not alone in wishing I had shown mine more love before having to have them removed*

THING to inspire me to start writing this puppy. Thank god for channeled rage, am I right? Ok sure, intense passion. Feel better?

So in my true oversharer, leave nothing to the imagination tendencies, I'm going to walk you through everything from start to finish with all the nitty gritty details — you ready, let's do the damn thing:

The day of...

My surgery didn't start until 10:30 AM so I didn't have to be at the hospital until 9:00. You're not allowed to eat anything after midnight the night before which I thought would totally suck as I always have 2 breakfasts, 'cause I'm fancy like that, but my nerves actually killed any appetite I may have had.

The morning of, I got up and took some time for me to journal and do some light yoga which really helped put me in the right frame of mind. I took a long shower, washed my hair (DO THIS) and rocked my surgical antiseptic wash. Mine was called Hibiclens — don't freak out when you open it and see that it's MF magenta colored like I did. And I proceeded to drink my required pre surgery apple juice and headed to the hospital.

When I got there, I registered and got set up in a private room to do all my pre surgery vitals and get my IV administered. I had to pat down my entire body with these cold wipes before putting on my gown — let me tell ya, the process was hella sexy — and then both my breast surgeon and my plastic surgeon came in, chatted with me and my support squad, and before I knew it, I was given my sleeping cocktail (which led to some seriously hilarious raw video footage of me thinking my body was a bowling ball and the bed's rails were bumpers) and got whisked away to surgery.

And then I blacked out. Literally. An entire 6 hours of my day was completely gone. One minute I was holding my husbands finger and the next minute, I was blinking half awake in the ICU saying that I was nauseous. I then blacked out again until I was in my room, surrounded by my support squad, with *Coco* playing in the background. A thoughtful choice on the one hand, given my love for adorable animated movies. I don't think they expected the sheer amount of tears streaming down my face as Miguel realizes Hector is Coco's real father.

Damn, Amanda, no spoilers! I know, I'm the worst. But really, if you haven't seen *Coco* already, you're a monster and you need to put this down and get that shit in front of your eyeballs stat. If there was ever a movie to Feel your feels to, it's that one.

The rest of my hospital stay was pretty uneventful. I was surprised how low my pain levels were (2/10), I was allowed to have broth and popsicles for dinner (which let me tell ya tasted DAMN

GOOD) and I spent the rest of the night/early morning watching movies, dozing on and off, talking with my support squad, taking meds and having my drains cleared by the nurses, who were a super wonderful and funny bunch.

Drains, you may ask?! If you've gone far back enough in my Instagram posts, you've seen the graphic AF video of them being removed from my body 9 days post surgery, but if you have absolutely no concept of what they are (which I sure as hell didn't before surgery), they're basically these bulbs that are attached to a long tube that goes into your body - mine were under my armpits - to help remove the post surgery fluid buildup. Glamorous, I know. And honestly, they were the worst part of the whole damn thing. Paired with my ability to do absolutely nothing for two weeks which, for an independent gal who loves spending her days filled with so many beautiful things on the go, was absolute torture.

My recovery process? It consisted of a hell of a lot of binge watching tv shows I had never watched (I got through six entire seasons of Game of Thrones), living in the same comfy pants for days in a row, wearing compression bras 24/7 (even to sleep), getting spoiled rotten with homemade food on the daily courtesy of my amazing husband and tea chats with my mom who came down to visit and help out for my recovery.

Because I was given nerve blockers at the time of surgery, I didn't need to be on any narcotics which was a blessing because this gal barfs them up like nobody's business. And let me tell ya, the idea of my surgical wounds healing and viciously vomiting did not sound like a pretty picture to me. (Psst, if you are gearing up for surgery, I highly recommend advocating for using nerve blockers. Best. Decision. Ever.)

For me, the drains were the most unglamorous part of the entire experience. They had to be stripped every couple of hours of fluid into the bulbs that looked like tiny plastic bombs on either side of my body. It is an extremely awkward task to try and do on your own so I was super grateful Kev was around to do it.

My timeline looked like this:

The morning after surgery, I was discharged from the hospital.

Day two post op, I showered for the first time with help. It felt better than all the orgasms and ice cream combined.

Day three post op, I looked at my new boobs for the first time and didn't have a complete breakdown. Huge win.

Day four post op, I had the worst headache of my life. Hot tip? Sleep with a plane pillow. You know, those cushy crescent shaped ones you always see at the airport and never buy? Trust me and get one. You have to sleep on your back for a minimum of two weeks on a propped up incline and the worst part will be your neck pain if you don't have proper support.

Day five post op, I got my pathology results back — no MF cancer.

Day nine post op, I got my drains removed.

Two weeks post op, I was cleared to drive.

Three weeks post op, I was cleared to walk my dog, go back to modified workouts and basically resume normal life outside of lifting anything more than 10 lbs.

And then life went back to normal right? Wrong. But you already knew that 'cause there's a hell of a lot more book to cover.

  Overall, the surgery itself was surprisingly the least scary part of the entire process. I had spent so much of my time leading up to surgery so incredibly anxious. Anxious because I had convinced myself that I was going to look like Frankenstein. That I would have a terrible recovery process. That I wouldn't be able to look in the mirror. That I would lose the woman I had spent so much time finally becoming proud of and grateful for.

And it turns out, the anxiety I created in my head leading up to the surgery itself was the most challenging piece to navigate.

Looking back at the surgery itself? It was just a blip on my radar. I sometimes go days completely forgetting that my foobs aren't my own and that I went through such a traumatic experience. You know, until I spill hot tea over me and don't realize until it hits my stomach. *Not having feeling in your boobs really throws you off. Especially during sex. More on that later.* But most days, I honestly forget…which in and of itself is a weird thing to say, but it's my truth.

Maybe you can resonate, and maybe the trauma or hard AF shit you've experienced sits with you every single day. Honestly, if it hadn't been for the tremendous support, positive coping mechanisms I had already been implementing in my day to day life and the surgical team that I worked with, I would probably be in a very different spot writing this. And yet, while I often find myself going through life as if "nothing ever happened", I still have constant reminders that no matter how hard I try, the reality of it is that things *are* and *always will be* different from here on out.

I've spoken to so many womxn on this journey — previvors*[12], cancer survivors, and thrivers, and every single one of them feel this immense pressure to "get back to normal".

Your hair grows back and you're good.
You're physically healed from surgery and you look normal, so you must feel normal too, right?
You finish chemo, find out you're in remission and you can finally go back to normal.

The reality of it is, **your old normal can never be your normal again**. You may look the same but you've been forever changed. It's like any traumatic experience in life — we endlessly look at our past selves as our *better selves*. I see this time and time again with my clients on the other side of trauma: womxn desperately trying to find the person in the mirror that they once knew. Can you relate?

I hate to break it to you but looking to the past to be a mirror to your future self is not only unrealistic, but a form of self sabotage. Tony Robbins says that if we aren't growing, we're dying. And I wholeheartedly agree. Every experience and challenge we face in life forces us to grow and uplevel. Are they often filled with experiences that make us yell "what the fuck world!"? You better believe it. But those

---

[12] *womxn like me who took preventative measures because of family history and/or a gene mutation

moments? They are pivotal in evolving into the person you were put on this earth to become.

When we spend so much time trying to come back to the person we used to be, we do ourselves a major disservice. We always need to be looking forward and the reality of it is that the person you once were is gone. And thank fucking God for that! Because this version of you is so much more layered, courageous and authentic. And I don't know about you, but I would so much rather show up and meet that version of you, than a shell of who you once were that you're desperately trying to become again.

Embracing your normal is the most radical act of self care you can do, my love. So dig in and let the new you shine through.

AND SO THE IMPOSTER SYNDROME SETS IN

I know, I know. You're eye rolling a bit with the ra ra-ing of the last chapter. I'm a seven on the enneagram,*[13] so I tend to see the world through a positive lens. Yup, just call me Positive Patty. I'll take it. I would much rather live in a world where I experience joy and light on the MF regular. That being said, I'm also a realistic human and I know that being joyful and happy go lucky all the time is impossible, and, truthfully, fake AF. And, more importantly, when we are fully feeling our feels and admit how sucky something is that we're navigating, we're able to make our way through it more intentionally.

A lot of my experience directly on the other side of my surgery was positive and filled with courageous acts. Getting in the car to go home, the first time I looked at my new breasts (what I so lovingly have dubbed my fuck yes foobs — *Fake boobs, get it? I knew you did.*), my first walk around the block to my first post mastectomy workout. They

---

[13] *The Enneagram is a super fun system of nine personality types that is based in modern psychology practices. I'm a giant personality test nerd (college me was the buzzfeed test queen), but I never felt like a description or result spoke to my soul the way discovering my enneagram number did. It's fascinating AF and I want to know yours - seriously, find me on social media and let me know.

were hella empowering to achieve. But I'd be lying if I said it hasn't been a MF rollercoaster of emotions and new feelings.

My biggest struggle post surgery has been one of major imposter syndrome. I have connected with so many incredible womxn navigating this journey, and the truth of the matter is that no story I've heard is the same. We all have gone through different versions of this path so there shouldn't be a comparison game, right? We all know it's not so simple. And while everything seemed pretty damn good on the outside -- I spent weeks doing nothing but lay on my couch, binge watching *Game of Thrones* for the first time with my incredible husband and mom waiting on me hand and foot amidst an overall pretty seamless recovery -- the imposter syndrome set way the fuck in.

The outpouring of love I received throughout my surgery and recovery process was incredible and honestly, overwhelming. In the best way. Don't get me wrong, I love me a good care package and the amount of boob themed cards and gifts I got was enough to fill me up for a lifetime. But you know when you have such an outpouring of love that even that can feel overwhelming AF? Yeah, it was overwhelm central in my world and let me tell ya, it was a lot to emotionally navigate. The amount of support was something I didn't anticipate and had so much appreciation for, but the amount of "you're so strong" and "you're a fighter" messages I received had me reeling. I have spent the last year of my life meeting so many womxn in the thick of triple negative breast cancer. Womxn who lost their mothers and aunts and sisters to this awful disease. Womxn who thought they'd beat breast cancer only to find out that it had come back and was metastatic*[14]. Womxn found their lumps in the shower and didn't have *a choice* — they were faced with a reality they never anticipated and became part of a club they never dreamed they'd belong to.

I, on the other hand, had a choice. My mom is still alive and well. My recovery process was record breakingly smooth according to my surgeons, and I was lucky enough to have insurance that covered most of the procedure. Was it my choice to have the BRCA gene mutation? No. But it *was* my choice to test for it. And it *was* my choice to take preventative actions to be able to avoid getting breast cancer in the future.

From my perspective, I was nowhere close to as strong or as much as a fighter as these womxn, and to claim those words for myself felt wrong. Because they had suffered "more" and "deserved to have the word fighter attached to their story". "My journey was nothing compared to theirs." There went my inner shit talker Jeanine telling me stories again. *By the way, have you named that pesky voice in your head yet? I promise you it's way more fun when you do.*

---

[14] *Did you know 1 in 3 womxn who have breast cancer will have a recurrence where it becomes metastatic? Aka a fancy ass way to say has spread beyond the breast and nearby lymph nodes to other organs in the body. Fuck, right? Not a fun percentage and one that I genuinely had no concept of before this year.*

I thought the feeling of imposter syndrome would go away, but those voices only got louder. And it all came to a head five months after my surgery, when I went to a camp for womxn impacted by breast cancer. In the past year, I've become a super active member of communities who advocate for BRCA and breast cancer, and the summer after my surgery, I went to a camp (think summer camp for grownups) specifically geared towards previvors, survivors and thrivers. I'm an extroverted person by nature, so I usually do pretty well in big group situations, and had been to many local events like this one. But this time felt different. Harder. And after some time away from it, I've realized that it was especially difficult for me for a couple of reasons.

I have a mixed experience with camp. When I was a kid, I went to an overnight girls camp on a beautiful lake in northern Canada every summer for 10 years. While I loved so many aspects of it, camp was also the place where I experienced one of the most traumatic experiences of my life. When I was twelve years old, I spent the entire summer at overnight camp being tirelessly bullied by the other girls in my cabin. Well, two girls, specifically. And it was torturous. At first it was a bunch of verbal bullying. Which, although incredibly difficult to navigate, was something I had had plenty of experience with in my life. I grew up as the headmasters granddaughter up until middle school when I

I CHOPPED OFF MY TITS

switched schools so...let's just say I had it rough. Being called names and being picked on? While awful, was something I was very used to.*15

One night, after the counselors had done "lights out" and left the cabin, the two girls who had taken it upon themselves to bully me that summer decided they were going to take things up a notch. Unbeknownst to me, and apparently my counselors, they had accumulated a bunch of rocks during the day and stashed them under their bunks. As soon as the counselor left, they hopped out of their bunks and immediately began to call me names and throw rocks at me. I screamed at them to stop, cowering into my sleeping bag to try to protect my head, but they wouldn't. Finally, when I felt the rock throwing slow down and thought I'd reached the end, I felt a canoe paddle and a broom hitting me, hard. I don't remember much more — our minds certainly do an impressive job of suppressing all traumatic moments we've had as a child to protect us. But what I do remember is covering my head with my hands and yelling at the other girls in my cabin to do something. Nobody moved.*16 I don't know what inside of me felt compelled to do this, but I somehow

---

15 *I in no means say this to downplay the scarring that comes from being bullied as a child. It's something I'm coming to terms with for the first time in my life thanks to therapy and let me tell ya, it's been sobfest emotional central in my house. If you are a victim of bullying, you are not alone sister.

16 *Truth? I don't blame them. I'm sure they're going about their lives and have their own trauma around this exact event. Guilt for not standing up and doing something. Or maybe they've forgotten about it entirely and are navigating their own mess. I suppose I'll never know. If you're reading this and are like WAIT I KNOW THIS GIRL I WAS THERE. I forgive you.

managed to muster up the courage to grab my pillow and run out of the cabin. I remember running as far as I could possibly go until I reached the lake, and when I turned around and saw they weren't behind me, I collapsed and started to uncontrollably cry.

I had experienced verbal bullying before, but nothing like this. And not only did it scar me from camp experiences, but it really put me on high alert around groups of womxn. Can ya blame me? From that moment on, I stuck with the guys, with the odd exception of gals here and there who snuck their way through (and still happen to be my best friends), but I *never* got involved with a big group of womxn until much later than life.

So yeah, camp was complicated as fuck for me. Don't get me wrong, I have so many positive memories from my summers away — like singing at the top of my lungs while sailing with my cousins and my best friend, getting a bullseye in every archery competition and watching the sunset and thinking about all of my dreams for my life. For the most part, I look back on camp with a whirlwind of positive memories. But, it's complicated, and, needless to say, the idea of going to camp again, 15 years later, gave me a lot of mixed feelings. So much so that I almost didn't go. But the overarching emotion won out in the end. I was excited to go. I had connected online with so many womxn who were going to be there, and I was excited to meet in person for the first time. And I knew that not going out of fear would be holding myself back from an experience that my heart and soul needed. So I went.

When I got there, in many ways, it was like coming home. I'd been to local support groups before and created so many incredible relationships with previvors and thrivers and survivors on social media, so to get to squeeze them in person and be surrounded by so many strong, authentic womxn who had all moved so many mountains in their life? It was incredibly impactful. What I didn't expect was to feel that imposter syndrome creeping in again after all of this time.

I had felt it before at my first in person meetup with womxn in the BRCA/breast cancer community. I had found out 3 weeks prior that I was positive for the BRCA 1 gene mutation, and I felt like my life had been flipped upside down. I somehow came across another woman with a story so close to mine on Instagram (there were very few twenty or thirty something womxn at the time openly talking about this at all), and she told me to come to this meetup — so I did. We met at a vegan restaurant in Chicago, and as we sat around the table, eating some vegan tacos*[17] and sharing our stories, I felt so overwhelmed. Every womxn around me had truly *been through it*. Either by battling breast cancer head on, getting diagnosed with cancer at an early age or womxn who also had the BRCA gene and had taken the courageous act of going through with

---

[17] *Seitan will just never be the same as good ol' grass fed ground beef for me. Sorry, not sorry.

a preventative double mastectomy. And there I was, a measly three weeks out of finding out I had the gene mutation, overwhelmed with my options and feeling like such a fucking imposter.

As I continued along my journey, that feeling of imposter syndrome? For a while, it faded into the background. I was *in it*. Seeing genetic counselors, making decisions, finding surgeons that supported my goals and values, and getting a date put on the calendar to officially go through with my double mastectomy. And as I continued to attend more local events, I felt more and more that I belonged, and that my story mattered. So when I found myself on day one of camp feeling like a total imposter, I did what any good mindset and wellness coach would do (seriously so damn grateful every day that this was my life's work coming into this mess) and I took a moment to myself to check in with where it was all coming from. The feeling of being an imposter? It was sparked the first night during circle time, a ritual where we go around and share our stories in a safe and supportive space. We did so that first night with our cabin groups, and of the twelve womxn in mine, I was the only previvor. I listened to these womxn talk about the first time they found their lump, having to watch their friends die from the disease and navigate survivors guilt, how fucking shitty chemo was and how they'd felt like losing their hair had caused them to lose their identity. And there I was, having never actually had cancer, and all around had a pretty seamless recovery from surgery.

I immediately felt so out of place and my mind was filled with thoughts like...

Who do I think I am sitting here?
Your problems are so less valid than theirs.
You should be grateful for having had such an easier time of it.

Maybe you can relate. Maybe you've sat in a room full of people questioning if you deserve to be there. If your story is important. And if you have, know that those feelings are so fucking normal. We've never been taught to believe in ourselves. Or given the tools we need to truly take inspired action and feel enough. Feel confident. Feel like we're living our fuck yes lives. *Don't worry, that's why I wrote this book sistah. You're in good hands.*

The truth that took me longer than I'd like to admit to actually believe? **My story is no less worthy than theirs. And neither is yours. It's just different.**

Have I faced immense hardships through this journey? You better fucking believe it. Different hardships. But they are no less valid. It took me a lot of work to sift through this and own that my story was worthwhile to tell. Because the truth is, I would have killed to hear a story like mine when I was going through the mess. I felt so alone. Like nobody could possibly understand what I was going through.

We spend so much time in hiding, believing our stories aren't good enough. Significant enough. And I know that now to be the farthest thing from the truth. I've had the pleasure of being able to share my story all over the place — on stage, on podcasts and in person. And every time I do, I look out into the audience and picture my pre-surgery self sitting there, with so much fear in her heart. And I speak my truth for her. Because I know how desperate she was for someone to share their story.

So how do we believe our stories are worth loving?

My dear friend so beautifully reminded me, when I was in the thick of it, that the beauty of this crazy thing we call life is that no matter what anyone else is navigating, the sooner we can find peace on our path, the sooner we will deeply see how innately worthy we already are. Self love is a concept thrown around a whole hell of a lot in this day and age, but so rarely actually defined in a way that resonates. For me, self love isn't an action as much as a feeling. Sure, bubble baths, pedicures*[18] and massages are nice and all, but it drives me crazy when others believe those are the only things that we can do to care and love for ourselves.

---

[18] *not manicures you heathen! Seriously, please help me understand the desire for gel manicures. I can't unsee the damage they do. I can't unsee it I tell you!

Self love is a state of mind, and the root of it is always self compassion.

Yes, you may quote me on that one. What does self compassion look like? To me, it's loving ourselves wholly - limiting beliefs, fears, doubts, insecurities and all. Self love is acknowledging that this journey we call life can often be HARD AF. Scary. Anxiety inducing. And lonely. I felt all of these things navigating my journey pre and post mastectomy, and a lot of people in my life couldn't understand what I was going through. Is it emotionally taxing? Yup. But it's also an integral part of the journey - to deeply experience all of those emotions, and then some. To take steps in supporting ourselves throughout the mess of it all. Implementing positive coping mechanisms, tools and finding communities that empower us along the way.

Do I still have days where I feel like an imposter? You better fucking believe it. I'm only human, despite my teleportation tits. *See what I did there? Bringing it back full circle 'cause that's what badass authors do.* But I'm learning that owning my story as valid and important, and traumatic for me - 'cause holy balls was it hard - is the greatest act of self compassion I could ever give myself.

MY STORY ISN'T OVER

The thing about a traumatic event is that you never really recover from it. I know, I know, it sounds fucking morbid, but it's the truth. Sure, you evolve. You grow. And you can thrive again! But it doesn't just magically poof go away the moment the event itself is over, like so many people often feel it should.

The saying "time heals all wounds" always pissed me off. Not because it isn't true. I believe that time is one of the greatest gifts when it comes to healing. *I mean, I don't usually remember what I ate for breakfast the day before. So, by that logic, I won't remember how or why I was upset about something three months ago.* Logic is clearly not my forte, but that's not why you're here. Ok, ok, Elaine, I'm moving on! What pisses me off is the expectations others have around the amount of time we *should* need in order to recover from something traumatic or hard.

Our relationship ends and we're given a few months to "get over it" before we move on, get back out there and try to figure out how the fuck the new world of online dating works…cue all the swiping and hoping to magically find our person based on looks alone.

We make it through chemotherapy, get told we're in remission and are magically expected to be able to "move on with our life" and get back to normal.

Our mom dies and we feel like a MF failure when the grief of it all is still weighing on us, a year later.

We go through a major surgery, rock out physical therapy and we look like we're all healed up on the outside so people assume we're "all good now".

As I'm sure you are all too familiar with from facing traumas in your own life, the truth of the matter is that it's never that fucking simple. And it can be frustrating as all hell when other people's expectations of our recovery timelines don't line up with our reality. All of a sudden, our minds get filled with a million shoulds…

Should I be further along?
Should I feel okay now?
Should I be able to just move on and forget the whole thing?
Should, should, should…

And we start to question our ability as a human being. We start comparing ourselves to that one girl on Instagram we follow who went through the same surgery and had a quicker recovery. Or who broke it off with her partner of 10 years the same month that we did and is already on the dating scene again.

We need to stop should-ing all over ourselves.

Seriously, if I could remove the word *should* from the English language, I would. I don't believe that anyone *should* have to do anything or *should* be expected to meet some arbitrary goal or deadline with anything in life, let alone when recovering from a traumatic event. We all have our own unique unicorn timelines. That's a fact that's simply not up for debate. Okay, Elaine?! Some people need a few months and they're back at it. Some need a year. 5 years. **The key here is that there is no wrong answer. There's only *your answer*.** And that is the accumulation of so many things — your history with trauma, your emotional intelligence, your personality type and beyond. Grief is a complicated thing and opens the door to super difficult emotions, and we all have different ways of dealing with it. I don't know about you, but when I'm going through something especially challenging, my first instinct is to run away from feeling *anything* around it. Seriously, I'll avoid it like the plague. My personality is wired for avoidance and numbing. Why do you think I spent so many years binge eating and over exercising? Thank you, brain!

It's taken years of work and therapy to learn how to truly *feel the feels*. Nowadays, I've gotten pretty good at actually leaning into my emotions and while, at first, it can make the grief feel a billion times harder, in the long run, it helps those feelings dissipate faster because the clarity on the other side of it comes a hell of a lot quicker. There was a time when my avoidance of my feelings was my number one objective, and I would spend months at a time going in and out of sadness, confusion, frustration, shame and guilt until it felt as if it ate me alive. Avoidance is where the majority of people find themselves immediately after something as sucky as this surgery. And most people stay stuck in that stage for a long long time. Sound familiar? You're not alone, sister.

Most of the recoveries you've watched from afar and find yourself wondering how they can muster to be so goddamn positive and how they've healed so quickly? I bet that if you were a fly on the wall behind closed doors, you'd see that it's not all sunshine and rainbows. Maybe they're putting on a brave face in public but in reality, they spend every night numbing out to a pint of ice cream and all the Netflix they can binge. Or maybe they're trying so hard to suppress their feelings to get by that they overcompensate with appearing joyful and as put together as possible. You never know what another person's truth is until you can peel back the layers and see firsthand for yourself — a privilege so few of us actually get in anyone else's lives but our own. So, in the spirit of pulling back the curtain and how rare it is to see the truth? I'm going to do just that. Holy hell, Brene*[19], the vulnerability hangover is coming, I can feel it!

My truth? There are days where I feel on top of the world. And lots of other days when everything feels like it's crumbling. Immediately after surgery, I intentionally took the time to really go through the healing process. And I'm not referring to the physical healing which was its own thing in and of itself. I mean the emotional healing of it all. I journaled every single day. I committed to seeing my therapist every week. And every time something came up that I was struggling with, I talked openly about it with my support system. And that's just the tip of the toolbox. I'm lucky. I had a MF leg up on most people going through grief and trauma — I'm a mindset coach after all. The tools I needed were already in my toolbox!

And I'm so fucking grateful for that. Grateful that I had the vocabulary and knowledge, thanks to the work I do in this world, to compassionately have navigated the mess of it all, but I'd be lying to you if I said that even now, I was 100% a-ok. Some days, I'm a complete and utter mess. And I'm blown away by the struggles I've continued to bump up against after all of this time. Damn you expectations!! If I'm

---

[19] *Yes, I just referred to Brene Brown on a first name basis. No, I do not personally know her, but mark my words we will meet some day. And if you don't know who she is, you must go read all her books and watch her Ted talk. Get ready to have your life changed forever.*

experiencing those feelings, you better damn well believe that everyone else going through trauma is feeling the same thing, or worse!

My point is? You're in MF good company, lady love. The next time you're walking home from work, crying your eyes out, mascara dripping down your face and screaming to yourself, "why me?!", remember that somewhere not too far away, another gal is doing the same damn thing. Knowing I'm not alone in navigating the mess of this all? It's comforting. Which is why I'm so damn committed to sharing my truth and my mess — I never want you to feel alone again. Because that girl walking home from work a total fucking mess? That girl was me. Truly feeling she was alone in it all while everyone else in her life magically had their shit together. **Reality check: Nobody has their shit together. Most people are just not willing to let their shit be aired in public.**

So welcome to the shit storm. The mess. The real, unfiltered truth of what it really looks like to sift through the crap and face your MF fears like a goddamn lion.

My story isn't over. It never will be. And, like it or not, this is always going to be a part of my story. And while I wish it weren't the case, this genetic mutation is going to impact my life's path in a lot more ways to come. Ways I probably can't even begin to fathom. Some amazing, and some probably devastating. Sure, I could spend my time stressing about all that's to come — hello anxiety! And some days, I do. I'm human. But through it all, I'm committed to moving forward by giving myself:

Compassion - to feel the feels, to sift through the crap on my own fucking timeline and be kind to myself when I feel like a hot mess express.

Time - to heal on my own terms, to fully flesh out all of the shifts and the mess attached to this part of my story.
And, above all, *the strength to rise up and be the goddamn warrior of my own life.*

Are you with me? Here we go.

PART TWO:

FACING YOUR FEARS HEAD ON

Well shit, ya made it to Part Two. The part where the meaty magic takes place and we deep dive into my second favourite F word — I'm sure you've guessed my favorite by now.*[20]

FEAR.

When you see that word, what immediately comes to mind? Maybe it's a fear that you have. Your frustrations around fear holding you back in your life. The desire to live your fuck yes life and be FEARLESS!!!

Side note: if your biggest fear in life is pigeons, we just became best friends. True story: I've had a pigeon fly into my head — beak to skull — three separate times in my life. No joke. It's been five years since the last encounter, but you better believe that when a pigeon is flying or even looks like it's about to take off, I will shove the person I'm walking next to in between me and it to avoid contact — even if that person is a stranger. You've been warned. That shit leaves a gal scarred for life.

Anyways, if you have a fear like my *very* understandable fear of pigeons, you're in good company. Hell, if you have any fears about anything in life, welcome home. This is not going to be your average

---

[20] *It's Fuck. But we all knew that.*

personal development book telling you all that be fearless and fear doesn't serve you ra ra ra blah blah blah bullshit! Hell fucking no.

That word, fearless? It's a complete crock of shit, if you ask me. Every time I hear it or see it written somewhere, I cringe and rock a major eye roll. Because the truth is that if we were fear - less, we would be royally fucked. Like biologically screwed. A sense of fear is a huge part of what makes us function as animals. The whole fight or flight *danger danger* response we have when we're in a precarious situation is literally what saves us from dying. From being trampled by the elephant that got out at the zoo and is stampeding towards us. Or in my mother's case, on Safari in Africa. *So glad you made it out alive, Mom, or my amazeballs readers would have never been able to read this gem!* Fear tells you to mother fucking run and get out of the way, which is exactly what my Mom did. Go Mom! Without it, she'd have been a squashed pancake. I'm no expert on the matter, but high school biology taught me that much.

Now don't get me wrong, I get the desire to not have to deal with fear. It can be a bitch. It can hold us back from doing things in life we really want to do but are just too damn scared to make happen... Asking for that promotion. Saying yes to that date. Starting a business. We *want* so badly to take the next step but are held back out of fear. Fear of failure. Fear of not being good enough. Fear of rejection...the list goes on.

As a society, human beings have a tendency to dismiss fear as weakness. Hell, I believed the same for the majority of my life. But I've had a major change of heart in the last few years and I truly believe that fear is not only vital to our survival, but an incredible indicator of strength. Fear, to me, is really similar to the way I view my anxiety — an intuitive gut check that tells me when I need to get curious about what the hell is going on and why I'm reacting the way I am*[21]. If we didn't have that response, we'd all be running around the world like psychopaths, not knowing what felt right or wrong from the vantage point of our own inner compass.

Now fear and anxiety are two different beasts. If I didn't say that here, my best friend, who also happens to be a psychotherapist and leading expert in the areas of mental health and anxiety, would kill me. But I think the idea of the feeling of fear or anxiety being this indicator to react is really fucking fascinating. Yay science!

Okay, back to fear. Let me tell ya, I certainly didn't always believe that fear was a vital part of life. My motto used to be "Fuck fear." As in doing my best "I am Sparta" Wonder Woman get the fuck out of my way fear impression as I ran through life. Can you picture it? As I've grown hopefully wiser (or at the very least had a shit ton more life

---

[21] *I am no anxiety expert, obviously. And I also understand that anxiety presents itself differently in everyone, but my research around this and speaking to leading experts in anxiety have all expressed similar findings so I'm going with it!

experiences that broke my naïveté in two), I've realized just how important the feeling of fear has been for my own journey. For one, without fear, we wouldn't have or need courage. And I believe that courage is the greatest act a person can make in their own life. It also happens to be one of my greatest values.

As Brene Brown*[22] says, "Only when we are brave enough to explore the darkness will we discover the infinite power of our light." I've seen this in my own life so many times. Hell, I bet if you really dig in to your own, you'll find the same. Think back to the moments in your life that you're most proud of. I bet you a million bucks and my entire collection of Grey's Anatomy old school dvds that fear played a part in it. That time you got up on stage and performed your spoken word poetry in public for the first time. Fear nobody would like it. Fear of being on stage in the first place. The first time you told your partner that you loved them. Fear they wouldn't say it back. Fear of getting too invested and getting your heart broken. That time you quit four of your seven part time jobs to start a business as a health & fitness coach even though you had no idea what the fuck you were doing...Fear. Fear. So much fucking fear. *And also so much bravery*. If fear wasn't present, that courageous action would just be an action. And I bet you in two years, you'd forget all about it, like any old run of the mill trip to the grocery store.

---

[22] *There's ma girl Brene again. I told you we were Bffs. Just because she doesn't know it yet, doesn't mean it's true.*

Plus, bringing it back full circle to my initial vote in favor of fear, having a fearful response is a very important physiological indicator of where we should be placing our focus. When we feel uncomfortable in life, fear often plays a part in that sensation. Growth? Personal development? Taking major steps that change the trajectory of our lives? Those are incredibly fucking uncomfortable and require a shit ton of expansion that can be down right terrifying.

So when we take a magnifying glass to the areas we are looking for growth and change — money, our love lives, our jobs etc — fear often rears its head like a crazy neon signs saying "Hey, I think you gotta take a closer look here, pal. You've got some work to do." It's when we have the courage to listen to that sign that our lives take shape the way in which we desire.

My personal and deeply passionate conclusion? Fear isn't the problem. **How we choose to handle the feelings of fear is the root issue.** When we make fear the enemy, we stay far the fuck away from situations and paths that could take us exactly where we're meant to go. Why do you think so many people end up living the same miserable life for forty plus years? They're too damn scared to do anything about it.

Well, I want more for you. Because we're all fucking scared. But that doesn't mean we shouldn't all be living our fuck yes lives. Are ya with me? Let's face fear head on and deep dive into all things FUCK YES.

In preparation for this book, I spoke with and surveyed so many womxn affected by breast cancer. Womxn who have the BRCA gene mutation like me. Womxn who have breast cancer. Are in remission. Going through chemo. Who thought their cancer had gone away and had a stage four recurrence. The works.

And I noticed a very interesting albeit unsurprising pattern in all of their responses — **fear steered the wheel in their lives**. Over and over again, I listened to the same fears being expressed. I could relate so deeply to all of them — and I realized that while some of the fears were specific to this community, almost all of them were struggles I have seen every womxn in my life navigate.

At the heart of it, every single fear was rooted in one of two things:

1. I'm scared that I'm not good enough
2. I'm scared that I'm not lovable

As human beings, we are programmed to desire two big things in life: purpose and connection. And when we believe we find proof that either of those two things are missing in our own lives, we feel an intense lack, and fear begins to take over. My goal with this part of the book is to remind you of a few things. For one, fear is a completely normal feeling. It's in our nature to experience it, and if you didn't have it, frankly, I'd be concerned. Second, and for the upteenth time because I can't say it enough, you are so not alone. And lastly, fear doesn't have to steer the wheel of your life forever. You ready? Let's do the damn thing.

FEAR:
MY BODY DYSMORPHIA WILL COME BACK

Do you remember the first time you looked in the mirror and thought to yourself, "I'm disgusting"? I do. I was six years old in ballet class*[23]. I was so excited to take the first step towards my lifelong dream of becoming a ballerina. I mean, hey, I was six and I had big goals. And this class was going to be my ticket to the big stage. It was all I could talk about for weeks - just ask my mom. The pink tights, black bodysuit and dreams of getting to dance in *Swan Lake* had me jumping for joy as I hopped out of the car and skipped into the building to take my very first dance class.

I walked in, head held high, kissed my mom goodbye and scurried my little feet into the studio. And before I knew it, what once seemed like the best idea of my life quickly turned into a nightmare. A group of girls, who had clearly known each other before the class, stood huddled together in the corner. As soon as I walked my cute butt into

---

[23] *I told you we were gonna get into the ballet story! I'm A MF woman of my word.

that studio, they stared at me and promptly turned to each other, laughing and going on about something.

At first, I didn't think anything of it and couldn't really hear their whispered back and forths. But then I heard one of the girls say the word "pig", and I looked over and saw that they were staring straight at me. I was stunned and didn't know what to think. The teacher promptly told us class was starting and I found myself at the back of the class, tears streaming down my face, attempting to do a first position plié and looking at myself in the mirror wondering for the first time in my life "why don't I look like them?". I spent the rest of the class comparing myself to the other girls in the class. I was taller than the rest of them by at least a foot. My belly pushed out and was noticeably bigger than the rest of theirs. The list went on and on…

And so the cycle of never feeling good enough in my body began, and my dream of being a professional ballerina ended. *Don't worry, I got back in the dance class ten years later, but that's a story for a different day.*

I spent so many years wanting to look into my mirror and magically see the body of my dreams. The one I thought I needed to have to feel good enough, pretty enough and beautiful. Ya know, the size 2 gal with perfect skin, blonde hair and tanned — you know, the one that every magazine has photoshopped to make us believe we have to look like in order to be happy. Hell, I tried to look just like her, for years. Dieted like it was my job. Spent hours at the gym. Became a crazy running cardio bunny even though I hated running. Ate bird food*[24]. Lost 30 lbs. Gained it all back. And day after day, no matter how I looked or how my body changed, I was endlessly let down with what I saw. It wasn't until I started doing the inner work and learned to actually love and appreciate myself that shit started to change and I could look in the mirror without picking every roll, stretch mark and bit of cellulite apart.

    Leading up to my surgery, I was terrified that my body dysmorphia would rear its ugly head again and that all of the inner work I'd done would be lost. And this fear is something I've had sooo many fellow womxn share with me too. It breaks my heart to say this, being a mindset and wellness coach myself. Hell, I teach my clients to love their bodies and feel confident and vibrant in their own skin once and for all. It's literally what I preach on the daily, and have gotten damn good at practicing too. Which, let me tell ya, this is harder than you'd think. So many of us teachers out there don't actually do what we say. It's my damn mission to do just that because otherwise, where's the MF authenticity am I right? Plus, loving our bodies in our day and age takes WERK, and you better believe I'm in the trenches with that shit right next to you sistah.

---

[24] *Kev seriously called my crazy dieting years my bird food years. I'd eat bird food during the day -- aka nuts, veggies and protein shakes -- and would binge behind closed doors at night.*

But the year before my surgery, my biggest fear in all of this would be that I hated my body. That I would look in the mirror every single day and be disgusted by what I saw again. That my self worth would be rooted not in my abilities, accomplishments or capacity for love, but my fucking clothing size and how good I looked naked on some arbitrary white man's scale of one to ten*[25].

Maybe you're in the same boat as I was and are terrified that you're going to look at your body in the mirror post surgery and spend hours crying, feeling awful about yourself. Maybe you got injured and are freaking out that your recovery is going to cause you to gain weight. Maybe you're reading this post partum and looking at your body, realizing that it's never going to look or feel the way it did before you got pregnant.

The reality of it is, all of those feelings? They probably will come out to play. Because we're all fucking human. And while it's far from the truth ('cause in case no one told you today, hot damn, you are beautiful just as you are right now), our brains are programmed to find proof that we aren't good/pretty/smart enough on the MF daily. Isn't that wild? It's like — what's it gonna be today? Couldn't fit into that pair of pants anymore? Ding ding ding! Proof I'm a big ol' fat lard. Can't do a pushup and I'm four weeks post surgery? Proof I'm never going to

---

[25] *damn my smash the patriarchy feminist sass came to PLAY. Sorry, not sorry.

get my strength back. Found a stretch mark on my hips? Call the doctor, find a cream to make it go away as fast as humanly possible because *goodness if we have an imperfect anything on our body.*

It's amazing what we've programmed ourselves into believing — but you know what's even more amazing? **That we have the power to change the dialogue.**

So...when these voices come out to play, as they always most inevitably do, how do we show up for ourselves with love?

We MF flip the switch.

That inner voice? Ya know, the one telling you you're too fat/ugly/need to have that inner thigh gap in order to be worthy? *Jeanine is back bitches!* That's the part of our brains that is searching for proof to back up the things it tells us are true about ourselves.

So that fear of "I'm going to feel terrible about my body post surgery"? As soon as I woke up and came out of the anesthesia fog, I immediately asked my husband how they looked because I couldn't bear to look down*[26]. And he said something along the lines of: "They're

---

[26] *not to mention I had all the bandages over it and was doped up from all the anesthesia and was far from coherent. Thank god he thinks I'm cute after almost 9 years. Yup, you guessed it, he's the real MVP here.

definitely swollen and there's some bruising but they look so much better than I thought they would at this point!"

Super sweet and caring, right?! ...What did good ol' Jeanine hold onto? The swelling and bruising — and freaking out that as soon as I looked in the mirror and saw them, I would never be able to accept my body as it was ever again.

This fear was so huge for me, but I had also done so much work to heal my relationship with my body. So, like the stubborn little shit that I am, I was committed to doing whatever I needed to do to not let my body dysmorphia cycle continue post surgery. This all started the day after I was released from the hospital. I was about to take my first shower and I decided to do the damn thing already and look. I was shocked. Shocked at the overwhelming feeling of pride and love that I felt in that moment. Were they swollen and bruised? You better believe it. My body looked like it had puffed up to twice its size. But all I could see was a woman who fought to take back control of her body. All I could see was courage. And I was damn proud of that.

That feeling continued for weeks, and I remember saying to Kev how surprised I was that I was feeling so good in my body. I wish I could tell you that feeling stayed with me, but I'm sitting here writing this six months post surgery and let me tell ya, it hasn't been that simple. Are there days when I feel so fucking incredible in my own skin? Hell fucking yes. But if we're being honest here, it's been a bumpy ride back to being happy with what I see in the mirror.

For one, my body has changed a lot since surgery, and I'm not just talking about my tits. Something I wasn't prepared for in the recovery process was how much my hormones would shift. I went off the birth control pill as part of my lead up to surgery. It was a personal decision. Not because I wanted to get pregnant any time soon but because I had been on it for twelve years after my doctor misdiagnosed me at 15 year old for PCOS*[27]. And in my going off of the pill and feeling very strongly about my desire to no longer be on any hormones, I decided to get the copper IUD. I've been off the pill for a year and a half now, and my body has taken a long time to readjust which, as I've learned, is completely normal. In fact, I didn't have a "normal" cycle until the two months leading up to my surgery. Side bar: Did you know that there is actually a pretty fucking wide range for what normal looks like in womxn across the board? According to my research this year, average cycles range from 21-35 days. That's a huge gap!

Anyhoo, when my body finally adjusted to a 28 day cycle and I could physically feel the shifts going through each phase, mentally and physically, I've gotta admit, I was pretty fucking pumped. When you're on the pill, you don't actually release and shed an egg (another fact that

---

[27] *Again, another story for another day. I've had some crazy medical shit happen to me.

completely astounded me when I started doing my research on going off of it), so I had essentially spent all of my life, outside of the first six months of getting my period, not ever experiencing my body working on its own.

As a health and wellness nerd who is obsessed with learning about the body, I was pretty stoked to see those shifts finally taking place for myself. But all of that changed after my surgery. Anesthesia can really fuck with your body's natural responses, and I didn't have my period for almost two months post surgery. And since then, my hormones and my cycles have been all over the place.

Hormonal imbalances or issues are one of the leading causes for weight gain in womxn, and since my surgery, while writing this, I've put on at least 15 lbs, despite continuing an active exercise regime and eating a balanced diet. And I'd be lying if that weight gain hasn't been frustrating for me. For one, half of my clothes don't fit. Thank god I work from home and can live in yoga pants and maxi dresses. And for another, I've found myself having more of those unhappy mirror moments than I'd care to admit.

And having this fear come true has been really fucking hard, especially when I preach body love and appreciation to my clients. I've had to take on my own tools more than ever, and I'm going to share a few of them with you right now, so that when you have a mirror moment, you can flip your fear to love.

So how do we flip fear and learn to love our bodies where they're at? **The key is to focus on what we do have instead of what we are lacking.**

Trust me for a moment and go with me on this, okay? It might feel like a crazy balls ask, but I promise you, if you commit to doing this today, you will start to see these shifts take place. You know that scene from *Mean Girls* where they're all standing in front of a mirror and picking their bodies apart?

Gretchen: "I hate my calves."
Regina: "You guys can wear halters, I've got man shoulders."
Gretchen: "My hairline is so weird."
Regina: "My pores are huge."
Karen: "My nail beds are not cute."
Cady: "I have really bad breath in the morning?"

I know you've had a Mean Girls Mirror Moment in your life. Hell, maybe you have a Mean Girls Mirror morning ritual without you even realizing. Well, it's time we flip that shit, stat. I want you to write on a bunch of post it notes things you love & appreciate about your body right now. Bonus if you write why you love them too.

For example: "My strong legs" / "My eyes" / "My booty and all the fun dance moves it allows me to rock out" / "My foobs for saving me from breast cancer"

Post all of your fear flip post it notes all over the mirror you look at most every day and strip down into your birthday suit. For ten whole minutes (set a timer!), stare into your mirror and say out loud every single thing you wrote down, over and over again. Look at every ounce of your gorgeous self and breathe in the body that allows you to move through life and give it some love.

Do I expect you to see every piece of you as beautiful right away? Hell no. That's un-fucking-realistic. But creating **Magical Mirror Moments** instead of Mean Girls Mirror moments will start programming your brain to become more self compassionate, which is the ultimate key to loving yourself as you are.

So take some inspired action today and rock a Magical Mirror Moment. Better yet, share it with me. Tag me @amandakatherineloy, email me, carrier pigeon me for all I care (which is a big fucking deal because I MF hate pigeons), and let me celebrate the shit out of your taking one step towards living your fuck yes life.

FEAR:

MY SEX LIFE IS GOING TO GO DOWN THE DUMPS

I like sex. A lot. I'll be the first one to admit that. It baffles my mind that sex is still considered such a taboo topic in our society. I mean..unless your'e asexual or a nun, if you're an adult, you're having sex. Maybe it's not *good* sex. And maybe you're not having it as frequently as you'd like or the kind of sex that really turns you on — I see ya kink community and I honor you and your leather ways — but you're having sex. So why does it have to be a big fucking elephant in the room? Fair warning: I'm going to be talking about sex a lot in this chapter. Sorry, mom.

Sex and physical intimacy is, in my opinion, a crucial component to any romantic partnership. It certainly is in mine. My husbands love language*[28] is physical touch. Mine is quality time, although my second highest is also physical touch. So when I say it's

---

[28] *If you haven't read The 5 Love Languages by Gary Champan, do it. It's so transformative in relationships of any kind, especially romantic partnerships.

important in my relationship, I mean that touch of any kind is a huge component of how Kev and I feel loved. And while obviously that doesn't just come down to sex, let me tell ya, if we've gone a while without getting it on, we start fighting about stupid shit like what to order for dinner. *Thai food. The answer is always Thai food.*

I didn't grow up talking about sex at all. And to this day, I'm not really sure why. I didn't grow up in a religious household. My parents certainly aren't sex negative. I just think they didn't really know how to address the topic beyond, "Are you being safe? Great." And the most I got from Sex Ed at school was a deeply rooted fear of getting pregnant after watching the most scarring video of a woman giving birth. My fourteen year old self still didn't know much about sex after that, but she certainly did know that she was going to do anything in her power to not get pregnant when she finally lost her V card.

My sex education came from personal experience. *Do I like that? Does that feel good? Who and what turns me on? What if he puts it in that hole?* And it's taken twelve years of exploration to figure out what I like. And most of the time, I felt alone in figuring it out, outside of playing around with my partner. Sure there was porn, but it didn't really do it for me. Let's be honest, most porn is geared towards men and is an unrealistic representation of how womxn experience pleasure in the bedroom...as are all of the romantic comedies I spent so much of my teenage-hood watching. Not to mention the erotic novels that are becoming more and more mainstream these days. I'm genuinely glad that series are being written all about the BDSM world and exploring your sexuality -- I'm all for breaking the barrier of things that have so long been considered taboo. But none of it actually prepares you for exploring your desires, sexuality and beyond in the real world.

Unfortunately still in our day and age, there aren't a lot of resources out there to truly understand the depths of what the sexual experience can be. That's why so many womxn rock missionary for the rest of their life and think an orgasm feels like a sneeze. How could they know any different? They haven't experienced anything else. And unless you're in a safe, supportive partnership rooted in honesty and where kind and transparent communication is the basis of everything, you're not going to have a safe container to explore.

All of this to say that it's no wonder this fear popped up over and over again with womxn in the BRCA and breast cancer communities. And not just that it would ruin their sex lives, but that it would downright destroy their marriages. Hell, I've seen multiple instances where womxn get diagnosed with cancer or choose to go through with a double mastectomy and it's the catalyst for their romantic relationships to end. Have you watched the netflix series *Dead To Me*? Christina Applegate's character had that exact same thing happen to her! Do I think it's the *only* reason for relationships failing? Hell no. But it's certainly a contributing factor, me thinks.

And while I'm no expert on the matter, licensed marriage and family psychotherapist and sex educator, Rachel Wright, had this to say on the subject:

It really boggles my brain that as a society, we haven't figured out how to talk about the very reason why we're all on this planet. Think about it; if you're reading this right now, there's a big chance that how you got here is from two people having sex. And yet, just the discussion of it makes a movie rating change, a parent to ask you to not talk about that in front of their child, or shame and feelings of guilt to come to the surface.

We need to able to talk about sex. Not talking about it is why when something scary is going on (like chopping your tits off or fighting cancer), it feels impossible to discuss it. If we can't talk about it when things are "fine," then how can we talk about it in an emotionally charged time?

Nowadays, I talk about sex openly with my friends. I share personal details around the subject on my podcast. Does it cause my numbers to go down? Maybe. But I want to live in a world where we are not just able to but encouraged to share about topics that get swept under the rug out of shame or fear of judgement. And the only way I know how to encourage that dialogue is to create safe spaces to have conversations around topics that are considered taboo.

And since we're on the subject of boobs, let's talk about nipples for second. *Did I make you uncomfortable? Nah, I didn't think so.* A not so fun fact about having a preventative double mastectomy? The likelihood of regaining any sensation in your breasts is very low. Now of course, it all depends on which surgery you decide to get — and there are lots of options! You can simply choose to remove the tissue and forgo any type of reconstruction. If you are a candidate, you can have a procedure called a DIEP flap reconstruction, a type of breast reconstruction in which blood vessels called deep inferior epigastric perforator (aka DIEP), in addition to the skin and fat connected to them, are removed from the lower abdomen and transferred to the breast pocket post mastectomy. Womxn will often opt for this route as a more natural option, although it does lead to a much longer recovery time as there is trauma not just to your chest but also your stomach. I actually wanted to go this route but I didn't have enough fat to be a candidate*[29]. Or you can go the route I went and have a double mastectomy with reconstruction, where implants are placed once all of the breast tissue has been removed.

What many people don't realize is that by choosing to go that route, I've completely lost sensation in my breasts. Zero feeling. And

---

[29] *Hush now, that wasn't a look at me I'm so skinny comment. Y'all know I hate that shit. You literally need enough volume of fat to be found around your abdomen in order to be able to make it work and if ya don't have it, ya just don't have it.

while to some, this might seem like it isn't a huge deal, this was something I was really worried about pre surgery.

My nipples were always one of the most sensitive parts of my body. And I used to find so much pleasure in nipple play during sex. So, I was super worried about how no longer having sensation in my nipples would impact my sex life. Not to mention my past with body dysmorphia and navigating the physical trauma of it all.

Unlike many womxn I spoke to, I never was fearful of these changes ending my relationship. I've spent the better part of ten years fostering a loving, honest and often overly communicative relationship with Kev, and I'm grateful for it every single day. Are things always easy? Hell the fuck no. Did this experience shift things for us? Of course it did. **The difference is that before and after the surgery, I let him in.**

As soon as my breast surgeon told me that I probably would never regain sensation in my breasts, I talked to Kev about it. I addressed my concerns around how that would impact our sex life and, specifically, how it would shift the way I experience pleasure when we were intimate. And after my surgery, once we got the go ahead to resume all activities, we took things slow and took the time to communicate about what felt good and what didn't.

Some of my friends who've had cancer especially struggled with the sex piece of it all. When you have cancer, not only do you (often) go through chemotherapy, but you're put on a protocol of hormone suppressant drugs. And as a result of those drugs, you essentially go through early on set menopause, which can lead to a serious lack of sex drive, pain with penetration and vaginal dryness. Super fun, right? Things you didn't think you'd have to deal with until your fifty plus and, instead, you're twenty eight and newly married. Seriously, my friends are rockstars. They deserve MF gold medals for being so fucking positive amidst this shit.

While all of the things listed above are physical things that need to be addressed (and can be, may I add, through a variety of means, toys, lubes, exploration in other ways etc.), the way to flip fear in this scenario, and in any situation in your life where sex isn't what you want it to be with your partner, is through one thing and one thing only: **communication**.

In my experience, most couples communicate terribly. And it's no wonder — we have never been taught how to effectively communicate with anyone, let alone our partner . You know, the person who society has dubbed as the person who magically needs to fit the bill as lover, best friend, co-provider, potential co-parent and roommate. That's a lot of hats to wear (and one I genuinely think is impossible to obtain — thank you world for creating the most un-fucking-realistic expectations which only lead to disappointment!), but when you don't have the skills to communicate well with each other, it makes shit really fucking hard. And my guess is that you're fighting about more than just what to eat for dinner. Or maybe you're not talking at all and suppressing all that shit until it eats you alive so much that you explode. Yeah…that one always works out so beautifully.

My point here around how we flip the fear switch around sex? Get hella fucking good at communicating with your partner.

But how do I do that, Amanda? Talking is HARD! I know, sistah. And I've found through my own personal rigamarole of communication hacks what to do and what not to do -- so you're welcome in advance for my misguided attempts leading to this goodness:

How to Communicate Like A Wizard

Follow these three tips for having an open and intimate conversation with your partner and I promise you, together, you can take on anything:

Express your feelings

This might seem like an obvious step but I know from personal experience that often, we want our partners to read our minds. "They should know their behaviour hurt my feelings." Oh yeah? HOW? Did you tell them that it did? Getting clear about your feelings and then having the courage to express them to your partner when they are in a space to receive it (aka not one minute before they're supposed to walk out the door to go to work*[30]) is a super important first step.

Now I will say that while I don't tend to believe in absolutes and usually stay clear from the terms "right" and "wrong", I do believe that there is a right and a wrong way of expressing yourself. The first thing to note is that your feelings are your own, and they are not caused by anyone but yourself. I know this may not be a popular opinion, but out of the many things we do not have control over in our lives, our feelings and our reactions to any external event are completely up to us. It took me a long time to own this one, personally. I used to use the "you made me feel" attack all the time when having conversations with Kev early on in our relationship. I quickly learned that while his actions may have been the catalyst to my feelings, ultimately, I was solely responsible for them. And furthermore, saying "you made me feel" immediately puts your partner on the defence, which is not conducive to a productive and kind conversation.

Instead of placing blame, put your feelings into words. Tell your partner that you are feeling scared or hurt or frustrated. That you are feeling guilty that you're having less sex than before. That you understand their desire for connection, and how frustrating that must be

---

[30] *been there, done that. Don't recommend it.

for them, but that sex has become more complicated now and that you would love to work with them to find a solution that feels good to both of you.

I have personally found that the best way to navigate challenging conversations is to use "I" statements. Ex: "I feel frustrated a lot lately. I'm tired of feeling like the person who does the majority of the chores around the house. It would really help me out if you could commit to taking on a few for yourself." or "I'm feeling really vulnerable lately and disgusting in my own skin and worried that you think I look like a monster now and will never be attracted to me again. I really want to be in a place to be intimate with you, but I don't know how to do that when I'm feeling like this. Can we work together to find ways to talk about this openly and find intimacy in other ways while I work through this?" Or whatever it is that is eating you alive! I've found that conversations like these really opens the door to having a productive dialogue that can actually lead to some form of a resolution, which is ultimately the goal. And if it's not…well, maybe rethink your relationships sistah.

Ask clarifying questions

This step is often for the partner who is listening to the partner expressing their feelings. So first off, do just that. Listen. Allow your partner to get whatever it is they need to off of their chest. If they're having a tough time doing so, or you don't understand what they mean about something, a great place to start is by using a simple phrase that has changed so much in my relationship: "Say more."*[31] This offers your partner room to elaborate without you saying the words "I don't understand." I don't know about you but every time I hear that from Kev, I immediately get sad and defensive. Something I've learned about myself is that I have a deep desire to feel seen for who I truly am. And when someone doesn't understand me or the reason behind my actions, it feels like a direct attack on me as a person.

Either way, being receptive to their emotions, confirming that you've heard what they've shared (perhaps by restating the feelings they expressed in step one), and then being willing to ask open ended questions is a huge piece of proper communication. Some examples of what you could ask: "What's the worst case scenario that could happen?" or "How can I best support you through this?" are wonderful ways of creating an inclusive dialogue around the subject at hand.

Be kind and show empathy

When you hear from your partner that they are sorry you're feeling this way and that you are completely valid in feeling the way that you feel, you feel better, right? Even if they don't necessarily agree with

---

[31] *Term I originally learned from Brene Brown. There she is again, that star!

your interpretation or the memory of the situation at hand, it feels fucking good to feel seen and heard.

Showing empathy comes easier to some than others. And ultimately, like expressing feelings and learning to ask clarifying questions, it's a skill that we can learn with practice. A pitfall I personally got into when first learning to communicate effectively was saying that my partner was wrong for feeling the way they felt. I may not have outright said "You're wrong!", but by stating that it was ridiculous to feel that way because that's not at all how something went down, or to simply negate their feelings by saying something like "well that's crazy, I'm going to love you even if you do have franken-tits!" isn't the way to go about it.

Even if you don't understand how they could possibly feel the way they're feeling, the reality of it is that they *do* feel that way. So the best thing you can do, when hearing about their feelings, is to say something like: "I understand how based on your perceptions and your fears around this, you could feel this way and I'm so sorry this has been eating away at you. I love you and I'm here for you, and while I will think you're beautiful no matter what your boobs look like, I totally understand that fear."

These three steps? They set the stage for productive, honest and kind communication. And have been huge for me in my own relationship — thank you therapy and my amazing friends Rachel &

Kyle at the Wright Wellness Center for giving me the launching point to cultivate these tools in my own relationships. You're the real MVPs.

Am I perfect in using these? Hell the fuck no. Thank you deeply engrained habits that don't serve me or my relationships! It takes work to adjust and reprogram, but it's MF worth it. These are fantastic tools for you to use in any situation in your life where you're feeling fearful or upset and need a set of tools to walk yourself through the mess. *I mean, expressing your feels, asking clarifying questions and then having some serious self compassion for yourself is pretty fucking great advice, if I do say so myself.* So there you have it. **Another way to flip that fear and take the courageous step forward: communicate like a wizard.** I promise you, one way or another, it will give you peace of mind and the answers you're craving.

FEAR:

IF I BREAK DOWN, THEY'LL SEE ME AS WEAK

I remember the day when I got the call that I was positive for the BRCA 1 gene mutation vividly. It was mid afternoon. I had spent my day on coaching calls, going for a long walk with my dog, Toby, and packing for my upcoming trip to LA. I was sitting at my desk, responding to some emails when I got the call. My heart was pounding out of my chest, and when I heard the words I already knew deep down were true, I hung up. I quickly called my husband Kev and told him, as stoically as possible, and then called my parents and did the same, and as soon as I got off of the phone, I started to sob. I ran from the office to my bathroom, stripping off every piece of clothing as I went, turned on the shower, got in, curled up in a ball at the base of the tub, and cried and cried and cried as the hot water ran over my naked body.

Kev came straight home from work as soon as he hung up the phone with me, and when he got back to our apartment, he found me in bed, wet, curled up in a ball and staring at the wall. And he laid there with me for hours. I couldn't move. My eyes stung from having cried so hard, and I didn't have the words to say much of anything outside "I knew it. I knew it. I knew it."

For the next few weeks, I found myself having so many emotional moments, but they happened *always* when I was alone. I've spent most of my life trying to numb my feelings. It often showed up in the form of using food as a coping mechanism or excessive control in the form of exercise, and I spent years on the binge eating and orthorexia train as a result. This time, however, my numbing took on the form of distraction. The day after I got the call from my doctor, I was scheduled to go on a two week trip to LA, San Francisco and Hawaii. So the next day, I packed my bags and got on a plane for a three day leadership business conference in LA. While there, I didn't talk to anybody about my results. I poured into the conference and put it as far out of my mind as I possibly could. It wasn't until Kev met me in LA for our drive up the coast to San Francisco that I let it back into my mind for more than a second.

Long drives are where Kev and I have our best conversations. It's like a vulnerability portal for us. Have something we need to iron out? Take a drive. Need to bring up a tough topic of conversation? Let's rock a road trip. And that drive from Los Angeles to San Francisco felt like the first time I had exhaled since the call four days prior.

As soon as we'd gotten the car out of the car park and onto the main highway and we knew where we were going, I finally gave myself permission to let the emotional floodgates open. The tears and the "why me"s came on strong, and all of the fears that had been going on in my head finally came spilling out.

Don't worry, Linda. I didn't cry for all nine hours. Kev distracted me and made me laugh so hard I inhaled my own snot and almost choked (you're welcome for that mental image) by coming up with some crazy idea of the creating of teleportation tits and how maybe, in the future, they would be invented for all womxn with post mastectomy implants and I could use my tits to teleport wherever I wanted to go in the world. *Told ya I'd tell ya more about this.* For real, this joke continued on for months. He even got me nipple stickers as a gift for Christmas last year that said "There" and "Back Again" and I laughed so hard I peed a little.

Showing raw emotions has always been a super vulnerable thing for me. Don't get me wrong, I'm a total sap and anyone who knows me knows that I tear up at any adorable rom com, videos of cute animals, and any time I get a homemade card from someone I love. But real, raw, messy emotion has always been something I've personally avoided by any means necessary. Did my attempts to avoid it at all costs always work? Hell no. Just like our beautiful drive up the California coast, Kev has seen me ugly cry more times than I can count. But every time

I've had an emotional response like that to anything, I found myself thinking that I should be stronger. That feeling things in that way was a sign that I lacked strength. And that's exactly how I felt as we pulled into San Francisco. "Get it together, Amanda. This is your anniversary trip. You can't be a blubbering mess the entire time."

So, in true old Amanda fashion who didn't work on embracing her vulnerability for the first eight years of her adult life, instead of owning my emotional truth, I opted to suppress it. It felt easier that way. I wanted to have an amazing time with Kev and spending the entire time crying wasn't my idea of a vacation. That car ride was the last time I cried in front of other people for months. Hell, I didn't even cry again for an entire week. The next time was a week later, that time I mentioned earlier in Hawaii on the beach. The tourists must have thought I was a crazy person, but I didn't care. I couldn't hold it in any longer.

The pattern of suppressing my emotions along this journey continued for longer than I'd care to admit. Sure, it felt safe to cry in front of Kev. He's seen me at my fucking *worst* and loves me for all of me. And my journal has seen more tears than most, so we go way back. And soon, the daily routine of working out first thing and listening to *This is Me**[32] and crying while I cooled down became a huge part of my process. But spending my time perpetually crying to friends, sitting in the suck of

---

[32] *Song from the movie, The Greatest Showman that you can't not feel MF empowered when listening to it.*

it all, and, god forbid, showing how fucking terrified I was online? I had never felt so vulnerable and it scared the shit out of me to let my guard down in that way. And with good fucking reason! We've been socially conditioned to believe that showing any type of emotion is a form of weakness. If you're a man*[33] and you cry, you're no longer seen as the tough, strong guy that you've been programmed to believe you're supposed to be. If you're a womxn and you cry, you're viewed as unstable, hysterical and unreliable. Is this global perception starting to shift? Yes. And yet these beliefs are so deeply rooted in our psyche. Emotions make me weak. A statement that while I logically know not to be true, I still often find myself feeling a lack of strength within me when I get "too emotional" about something.

      This was something I felt deeply throughout my lead-up to surgery. So many of my family and friends told me how impressed they were with how well I was handling what I was navigating. That I was so strong and courageous for everything I was doing and how I was showing up for all of the doctors appointments, decisions and beyond. When in reality, I felt like a total fraud.

Would they still think I was strong if they knew I was having daily breakdowns behind closed doors?

---

[33] **** *know this is a gross stereotype and not always the case but let's be honest, stereotypes exist for a reason. And yes, I mean any male identified human or even male passing human (aka a person who to the external world passes as a man, not a womxn).*

If I shared how I was truly feeling and how much anxiety I was going through, they would feel differently.

These thoughts whirled around in my head for months, and throughout that time, I realized that by not sharing how I was truly feeling, I was doing a disservice not just to my community, but to myself. Being a public figure*[34] is what truly forced me to break my own personal stigma around appearing weak and feeling my feels. Why? Because the thing I thought about after I got the call from my doctor, immediately after thinking: "I knew it" was "how can I use this for good?"

I believe that we are given mountains to overcome in our lives for a reason. And I quickly discovered that my reason was to use the gift of my online platform to help other womxn in my shoes feel less alone. Because let me tell ya, in between the traveling and exploring the mountains in Hawaii, I was spending my time desperately searching for someone my age who was going through what I was too. I like to consider myself a social media ninja — it's a huge part of my job, after all — but other than a few Facebook groups that consisted of mostly 50 year old womxn and up who had already had kids and were in a completely different phase of their life than I was, I came up short. Podcasts about it? None. A book about what it's really like? Nada. I found the odd

---

[34] *I know, I know, I hate that word too but y'all cannot catch me ever using the word influencer. Gag me.*

Instagram post and blog post about it but most of them outlined tips & tricks for surgery and packing lists for the hospital.

I craved real and honest conversation. I wanted to see another womxn just like me sharing vulnerably about what it was really like for her, so I didn't have to play a shit ton of guessing games. So, in true Amanda fashion, I decided to be that person. My podcast, *Live Your F*ck Yes Life*, had launched literally two days before I got the call, and while I had no intention of using it as a platform to share my story around BRCA (ya know, since I didn't even know that I was positive), once I had settled into my reality, I recorded my first solo episode about what I was going through, in real time*[35]. It was fucking terrifying to let that episode go live, but I'm so grateful that I did because it captured my true emotional state at that part of my journey.

Sharing my story is how I flipped my fear into purpose. Is showing up vulnerably about this part of my life scary and hard? You better fucking believe it. But I knew that if I could change just one person's life for the better, it was worth it.

Now, I'm not saying that you should go out and start a podcast, write a book or make a zillion social media posts about the trauma you're facing in your own life. Our paths are all different and, for

---

[35] *If you're curious, go back to episode 6. It's a goodie.*

many of us, sharing our stories in such a public way is the farthest thing from the right path for ourselves. But if my obsession of self development practices and the past year has taught me anything, it's that vulnerability and being willing to get in touch with your emotions is the true definition of strength. Owning the emotional parts of this journey gave me strength that I never imagined possible. And it turns out that my big fear about being perceived as weak got totally blown out of the water. If anything, sharing my story has been the vehicle for others to unlock their own strength from within. And while I am still taken aback by it, so many womxn have heard my story and seen my vulnerability and reflect that they see nothing but strength, courage and a true warrior in front of them.

I echo those words back to you right now sister. Because no matter what darkness your facing, that is what makes you so damn worthy and strong to me.

So, how can you flip this fear on its head? **Share your story.** It doesn't have to be online for the world to see, unless that gets you hella excited, in which case, go for it. The world needs to hear your voice. It can be as simple as opening up to a loved one. A friend. Your partner. Writing a letter all about what you're going through that you never actually send, but allows you to get that shit out of your head and onto paper. Your tears are beautiful, lady love. Your emotions are so fucking valid.

Anxiety is a super typical response to any traumatic experience in life. Every single person I interviewed for this book experienced anxiety in some capacity. Some in greater ways than others, but they all felt it. And I hope in reading this, you are reminded that you are not alone. It can be so fucking overwhelming to navigate your emotions, especially when we're told to put ourselves last in life and just "suck it up and deal with it".

So this is your official permission slip, if you need it, to let yourself feel it all. Because that, my love, is my definition of true strength.

FEAR:
MY LIFE IS NEVER GOING TO GO BACK TO NORMAL

A couple of years after college, while on the outside, my life looked pretty damn good, I was in total shambles. I got my degree in musical theatre, and while I was lucky enough to be consistently employed as an actor since graduating, I still had to work a shit ton of day jobs to pay the bills. I love acting. Being on stage and singing and performing to an audience is one of my favorite things to do on this planet. It feels like home to me. But the reality of it is, unless you're a movie star or incredibly fucking lucky, you are basically working for the love of it, not to live.

I knew that this would likely be my reality. My professors had prepared me to live the struggling actor life and get a day job that was both flexible and paid enough to cover my living expenses. And by 2015, I found myself working seven part time jobs just to scrape by. I taught theatre and piano lessons, I babysat, I worked as a Segway tour guide*36, had a brief stint at a call centre and, of course, I was going to auditions, rehearsing and performing. Sometimes even working on multiple productions at once. So I'd run out the door at seven in the morning, and bounce around to my multitude of jobs (*the color coordination on my planner was prime, let me tell ya*), scarf down dinner in my car, go to rehearsal, get home at eleven at night, only to pass out and do it all over again the next day. All while simultaneously planning a wedding and finalizing buying an apartment in Chicago*37.

I was fucking exhausted and living pay check to pay check. My anxiety was at an all time high. I was having panic attacks every week. I was stressed, overwhelmed, in the prime of my eating disorders and spending most of my time "off" in the car, commuting between gigs, screaming at the top of my lungs at the "idiot drivers to go fuck themselves".

I know, Nancy, I wouldn't have liked me either. Like I said, I was not in a good way. And I certainly wasn't the positive person you now see in front of you. For the record: having a positive mindset does not come naturally to me. It takes a shit ton of work for me not to be a negative downer, and sometimes, despite my best efforts, I can get stuck

---

36 *It's not as fun as it sounds. I mean, the Segway-ing is. Do it if you haven't. But tip your tour guides for the love of all that is holy.*

37 *For the record, I do not fucking recommend this.*

in that negative cycle if I'm not careful. But I spent so much of my life living that way and I refuse to put my energy there anymore, so I work damn hard to avoid it at all costs.

The crazy thing is that at the time, from the outside looking in, my life looked incredibly put together. I was checking all of the boxes of what we are made to believe we need to be able to experience real happiness. I was in a loving relationship and getting married to the man of my dreams. Check. We were buying our first home together. Check. I was doing what I loved, and what I went to school for. Check, check, check. Sounds pretty shiny, right? Now don't get me wrong, this isn't at all a woe is me feel pity for the privileged cis gendered upper class white girl act. I own that I come from a hell of a lot of privilege and I've been incredibly blessed to have the opportunities I've had in my lifetime. What I'm trying to illustrate is that shiny superficial markers of success don't automatically equate to happiness. I finally had the partner, the house, the dream shows to perform in, and I still wasn't happy.

That post married not so blissful moment when I realized this felt like deja vu all over again to two years prior. To the first time I went on a diet, exercised like crazy, lost 30 lbs, and finally got down to the coveted size 2 diet culture had primed me to believe was the path to true happiness. And when I got there, not only did I still feel miserable, but I was undernourished, incredibly unhealthy and exacerbating the inevitable yo yo dieting cycle that I had found myself on for the better part of ten years. Been there too? Like I said, you're not alone.

What I know now is that **the real reason I wasn't happy had nothing to do with my external circumstances, but everything to do with my relationship that I had with myself.** And let me tell ya, it was pretty fucking shitty. That inner voice in my head? Jeanine? Often referred to as the inner critic, shit talker or what have you? She ran the show. I spent so much of my life worrying about what others would think of me that I dimmed so many pieces of my true self that when I looked in the mirror, I couldn't recognize the womxn who stood before me.

When I started doing the inner work and deep diving into the world of personal development, journaling and beyond, I started to slowly peel back the layers of my true self. It takes a lot of work, uncovering and questioning, and you better believe I still have a long way to go, but the womxn I'm showing up as today is one that, for the first time in my life, feels like the authentic me.

She unapologetically lets her freak flag fly.

She says the word "fuck" more than the average person.
She is actually pretty driven by spontaneity and adventure, despite having identified as a type A perfectionist for the better part of her life.

She says the honest truth of what is on her mind instead of what the other person wants to hear.

She says no to things unless they're not a MF hell yes.

She laughs so hard she snorts, sings all of the time, doesn't believe in anything but giant bear hugs when saying hello, and treats her dog like her child.

And I really fucking like her. This new normal Amanda rocks my socks off, and while I know that I will continue to inevitably grow and evolve*[38], as all human beings do, the foundation I have built and the limiting beliefs about myself that I have shed are things I'm incredibly proud of, and equally terrified to lose.

I remember the first time I had this fear pop into my head — that having the BRCA gene and going through with this surgery would mean my life would never be able to go back to normal — it completely took me by surprise. I was sitting on the dock one morning at my family's lake house in Canada. It was exactly the six month mark countdown to my scheduled double mastectomy, and my three best girlfriends and I decided we needed to have a bon voyage to the boobs weekend.

---

[38] *read: fuck up royally

My cottage is my favorite place in the world. It's the one place in the world where I can go and feel fully and completely myself and at peace, no matter what is going on in my life. And I knew that spending time up there with my favorite people on the planet would be exactly what my heart needed. What I didn't realize was how much processing would take place in those few days. I laughed, I cried, I had an amazing topless photo shoot to commemorate my pre-surgery tits, and I expressed my fears out loud for the first time: "What if I never go back to normal?" I loved this version of myself. I was proud of her. And I was absolutely terrified that once I had had the surgery that all of my fears and limiting beliefs would come back. Or worse, that I wouldn't be able to recognize or like the me on the others side.

I'm not alone in this fear. Hell, I bet that you've had this fear pop up in your life more times than you can count. It could be as simple as holding onto that pair of jeans that haven't fit you for years because you're hoping you'll be that size again. Or maybe the person you've spent the last seven years dating and that you plan on marrying dumps you out of the blue, and you wonder if you'll ever love or trust another person again.

My friend Leanna Blanchard and I met because of this whirlwind of a journey. She's my age, and around the same time that I was finding out I had the BRCA 1 gene mutation, she was finding a lump in her breast and hearing from her doctor that she had breast cancer.

She's done it all — the chemo, the hormone suppressants, the countless doctors appointments. Cancer has taken over her life and, in many ways, she's felt that it's put her life on hold. While the rest of her friends are settling down and having kids, something she very much wanted for herself, she's been spending her days fighting to stay alive. And she's kicking cancers ass, by the way. Seriously, she's a fucking badass and I'm so grateful to know her. We've talked a lot about her feelings and fears that she's navigated as a result of her diagnosis, but through it all, the one thing that kept coming up over and over again in our conversations is her desire to have life "get back to normal".

Here's what she said about her experience navigating this fear:

I remember when I was first diagnosed with breast cancer, I thought to myself: "Okay, it'll be one long year of chemotherapy, surgeries, possibly radiation, etc, and then I'll be back to my life and I'll move on." I was 28 years old, had been married only six months, and had just a few weeks to go to complete my physical therapy fellowship. I didn't have time for this, and I planned to let cancer affect my life as minimally as I possibly could. I didn't think support groups were necessary, and I just wanted to power through.

As I approached the end of my six rounds of chemo, I started to realize that things weren't feeling like they'd easily get back to "normal". But I pushed those feelings aside for the most part, joined a few support groups, and resolved that after my surgeries I'd feel normal again. After my mastectomy and reconstruction, finding out that I wouldn't have radiation after all, and starting on my anti-hormonal therapy, I had another nagging feeling that I wouldn't really ever get back to normal. But yet again, I pushed those feelings aside.

It wasn't until I approached the one year anniversary of my diagnosis that it really started to hit me - I wasn't EVER going to have my old life back. I wasn't ever going to "get over" my diagnosis. That anniversary passed, and then the one year mark of completing chemo snuck up on me. I was thankful that I finally had a decent head of hair, but it was yet another stark reminder that even though it had been a year since I pumped toxic chemicals into my body to try and save my life, I didn't feel any less broken.

When I finished chemo, when I healed from both surgeries, and when I reached one year post treatment, I can't even tell you how many times I was asked, "So you're okay now, right? Like, you're done with everything?" Oh, how badly did I want to put a smile on my face and say, "Yes! I beat it - I feel powerful and as good as ever."

But the fact is - that just doesn't happen.

Even if you take away the fact that I'll be on estrogen and ovarian suppressing medications for the next 5-10 years, there still isn't a return to "normal" after completing cancer treatment. I frequently hear the phrase "new normal" thrown around, and to be completely honest with you, I HATE that phrase. I don't want a "new normal", I just want my old life back. I want friends and family to recognize that though I am past a lot of the really hard physical treatments and milestones, it doesn't do any of us any good to compare who I was pre-diagnosis to who I am now. I am the same Leanna, but my world is forever changed. The pressure to get back to work, to a typical marriage and to regular social outings is overwhelming. No matter how much people love you and no matter how well they mean, any reference to returning to normalcy is hard to swallow. Everyday I find something new that cancer has taken from me. Just when I think I've processed all the grief and trauma, something else comes up. It's heartbreaking.

All this to say - I am grateful to be alive. I don't hate my life. I'm lucky to have this second chance to try and discover more of what makes this life worth living. Normal isn't something I think I'll ever really feel again, and everyday I will work on coming to terms with that.

Bring out the MF tissues, am I right? I have so much respect for Leanna. And she, as always, makes a super fucking important point. We spend so much of our lives trying to go backwards. Live as we *were*. Find the way we used to be. Look the way we used to look. Feel as happy, care free and spontaneous as we used to feel. And, as a result, we move forward in life, constantly living for the past instead of moving towards the future. When we do this, life feels pretty fucking abysmal. And the cold hard truth of the matter is that finding that "normal" is impossible. It's not yours to find anymore. It's three stepping stones back from where you are right now. And those stones in between? Those moments that have impacted and defined your life in profound ways have changed you.

Maybe they're moments that have been tough to navigate. Rocked you to your core in ways you never imagined and the trajectory of your life is radically different than you wanted it to be. In any case, this? The circumstances you're living right now is all that matters. So why not learn to embrace what is?

Cancer fucking sucks. Living with a genetic mutation sucks. Losing your job, getting divorced, having a loved one unexpectedly die — it all stinks a giant pile of dog shit. *And* it's a part of our story. It shapes the lens through which we see the world and how we choose to show up everyday. So when we try so hard to get back to the way things used to be, we're paddling so hard upstream on a river with mother fucking stage four rapids.

What if, instead of putting all of our energy into something that will *never* get us anywhere, **we chose to ride the waves and go with the flow**. Is it scary? Hell yes it is. We knew what that old normal looked and felt like. The next step and where we're going? It's uncharted territory. The unknown can be hella terrifying. But it's also incredibly freeing.

A huge takeaway I've learned from all of this is the importance of looking forward. Making the decision to do so has been a total game changer for me. There's a lot in our lives that we have no control over. What we do have a say in is the way that we think, how we choose to respond and feel, and the way in which we show up for our lives. And every day for the past two years, I chose to make the decision to look forward instead of looking back.

When I decided to go through with my double mastectomy, did I *want* to do it? Hell fucking no. If my circumstances were different, there was no way in hell I would have ever gone through with it. But I knew my reality, understood the odds, and made a decision looking forward to the rest of my life, instead of trying to hold onto what was.

And you can do the same. **We flip the fear of losing ourselves by remembering to let the flow of the stream move us.** Every stepping stone and obstacle that we face along the way is helping shape us. You are not a tree. So move, sister. It's all a vital part of the growth process.

FEAR:

I'M GONNA HAVE FRANKEN-TITS

I was never particularly fond of my boobs. They were pear shaped and pointy and the amount of nipple hairs I had on the regular were impossible to keep up with. Spoiler alert: you still get nipple hairs after a mastectomy. *Yeah, I know, I was not prepared for the continued plucking either. Silver lining: at least now I can't feel the uncomfy AF sharp sensation when I tweeze. You're welcome for another super sexy visual.*

Growing up, I did everything I could to change my boobs. All of the other girls in my class had already "developed" and had gone bra shopping with their moms. And when the most popular girl in school's boobs really popped, all of the boys came running. And there I was, 14 years old and still rocking a training bra.

When my boobs finally decided to show up, and I bought my first Victoria's Secret B cup bra, as all the girls in my class had, I was ready for all of the boys to come to the yard, and let's just say...my milkshake didn't work. Apparently, neither do jeweled push-up up bras

I CHOPPED OFF MY TITS

that never see the light of day by anyone other than my mom and the very nice salesperson who sold it to me. *Side note: Please tell me you know that Kelis song reference or I will officially feel like an old lady. That song was my middle school attempt to shake my booty and have my crush fall in love with me. It didn't work, but you better believe I worked it.*

I thought if I found a way to squish my boobs together enough so that they'd make that ever so desirable cleavage I'd heard so much about, all of my love life woes would go out the window and my best guy friend would finally fall in love with me. Turns out, no amount of boob shape shifting was going to help that one. If I could go back in time and talk to my fourteen year old self, I would tell her to stop worrying so much about how my boobs looked and just confidently be myself.

As womxn, we're made to believe that our boobs are our prime symbol for sexuality*[39]. I've never understood why people go bonkers for boobs. I mean, they're just lobs of flesh and fat that bounce in weird ways and can be kind of a pain in the ass. Or back, if you're one of my D cup and up gals. And yet men (and many womxn) go fucking crazy for them.

---

[39] *My best friend would disagree with me on this one and say that our entire body looking a certain way is a big part of what is deemed "sexy" and while she's certainly not wrong, I'm making a MF point so go with me here.*

The first time a boy touched my boobs, I thought it was going to be this magical thing. Second base, holy shit! I couldn't wait to tell my friends. But beyond the novelty of having a hand cupped around my breast for the first time, it was pretty lacklustre outside of the fact that it was with my first boyfriend who I really liked.

The irony of the fact that I chopped my tits off, and how desperately I didn't want to do it, is that I never liked my boobs. And I have no scientific evidence to back this shit up, but from all of the times I've spoken to friends about it, 95% of the womxn I know — the 5% reserved for my best friend who thinks she has the nicest boobs on the planet and could very well be right, I've seen 'em — hate their boobs too.

Boobs come in all shapes and sizes. We are all made differently, and yet we all find something about them to pick apart. *They're shaped weirdly. They're too big, too small, too pointy, too soft. Our nipples are too big. Our areolas look like pancakes. The list goes on and on...*I always hated my pointy pear shaped boobs. And yet the moment I decided to chop 'em off, I wished I had spent less time complaining about them and more time loving on them.

A huge attempt in celebrating my breasts pre-surgery was through a bon voyage to the boobies weekend and photo shoot with my best friends. I went into the weekend with the intention to celebrate this next step, show my body some serious love and do something playful and fun to mark the end of a chapter and the start of a new one. I was shocked at how liberating it felt to not just take the photos, but to see the end result on camera. Instead of looking at my breasts and picking them apart like I had done my entire life, I found myself reveling in the beauty of my body. And while they very well could have killed me if I hadn't taken preventative steps and removed them, instead of looking at them as ticking time bombs, in that moment, all I could see was a beautiful snapshot capturing a moment in time that I will forever be grateful for. For the first time in my life, I found myself getting sentimental about my boobs. I had spent my entire life not really caring about my breasts and now, all I could think about was what they were going to look and feel like after my surgery.

The internet is a scary place and one that honestly did me very few favors in my decision making process and prep for surgery. Instead of helpful articles, I found worst case scenario sob fests. Instead of uplifting photos of post surgery bodies that looked normal and healthy, I saw photos so horrifying of botched surgeries and disfigured boobs that I can never unsee. I was so terrified my boobs would look like Frankenstein had ripped them apart and sewn them back together. That I would hate my scars and feel like a monster. And I had good reason — my breast surgeon told me to expect that, at least for the first few weeks post surgery! So I went in expecting the worst.

What I never anticipated was falling more in love with my breasts than ever before. Not for what they look like (although my surgeons knocked it out of the park), but for what they represent.

When I look in the mirror today, I see courage. My scars are a reflection of the strength it took for me to decide to be a warrior instead of a worrier. Does the fact that when I lean forward my implants ripple under the skin and you can see that? Sure, it's weird. But I'll take ripples over cancer, any day. I'll be the first to admit that I had one of the more positive recovery processes I've heard of, and am really happy cosmetically with the outcome. Not all womxn have similar experiences. And while some of this is out of our control and dependant on our bodies, I truly believe that a big part of the end result is in our hands.

For one, my surgeons were blown away by my recovery process. I was back to business, almost as if nothing had happened, three weeks post surgery. I had no complications, no infections, nada. When I asked my doctors why my recovery process had been so quick and unheard of, they told me that it had everything to do with my healthy habits leading up to surgery.

I spent the nine months leading up to surgery as if I was prepping for a marathon. I intentionally focused my workouts on muscle groups that I knew would need to be stronger for my recovery. I fueled my body with nutrient dense foods, got my gut health in tip top shape and amped up my supplement and water intake so my skin and organs were thriving. I also did my homework and due diligence in choosing a surgical team I trusted. Luckily, Chicago has some of the best surgeons in the country, and I spent 3-4 months meeting with as many breast and plastic surgeons that I could. I wanted a team that was honest. That allowed me to advocate for myself and hear my thoughts and concerns. That were masterful at what they did. And I wanted to walk into the room and immediately feel comfortable. My team did all of that for me and more and I attribute them as a huge factor to my healthy recovery and overall happiness with my experience.*[40]

Like any big decision in your life, it's always important to go into it prepared and with your best foot forward. In my opinion, that looks like asking for second, third and fourth opinions, not taking anything at face value, and advocating for the things that are important to you. I've spoken to so many womxn who went through this surgery without realizing that they had any option other than what the first surgeon they spoke to outlined. Who had no concept of the benefits of exercise, nutrition and positive mental health coping mechanisms throughout their journey. Who were told that the option to reconstruct their breasts was off the table and went flat, even though they didn't want to, because they hadn't asked for a second opinion and didn't know any differently.

---

[40] *If you're in the Chicago area and want to know what team I used, reach out.*

When I was bopping around to various surgeons offices to have initial consuls, I had one surgeon tell me that I would have to go through an exchange surgery (instead of what I did, which was direct to implant (DTI)), even though I had seen three other surgeons who had told me I was a perfect candidate for direct to implant, my preferred method. When I challenged him on that, he stuck to his guns, and obviously I didn't choose him. I later learned from others in my local community that this surgeon is notorious for saying no to the DTI option because he, himself, isn't comfortable with it. Which, for the record, is totally fine! While I wish he had come outright and said that to me, I appreciate him sticking to his guns and advocating for his personal practice. That being said, had I simply gone to this man and trusted that what he was telling me was the capital T truth, I would have gone down a path that wasn't right for me.

My best advice for flipping your fear around this is to **take action centered around your biggest asset, your gut**. If you have an inkling that something doesn't feel right, it probably isn't. If you are feeling pulled towards something and you can't explain why, move in that direction anyways. And, above all, take action.

You don't want your tits to look like Frankenstein? Cool. Do your research, hire coaches that will support you on your mental and physical health journey and choose a team of doctors who's results you've seen and match what you're going for. And, girlfriend, if you feel like it's too late and your worst fear has come true and you spend every single day of your life feeling like MF Frankenstein, remember this: Your scars are the reason you're still here. And if that isn't something to celebrate, I don't know what is.

FEAR:

I'M GOING TO DIE

I promise you this chapter isn't morbid. The title is ominous, I know, but hey — I'm here! Living and breathing and writing this to you ask we speak, so we know that I'm alive and well and that this fear didn't come true. I am a gal who tells it how it is. I don't believe in leaving out the mess, the emotions or the fears. I spent too much of my life trying to be perfect and putting up a front to do that now. It is my mission in life to show up as candidly and honestly as humanly possible, and I'd be remiss to leave this chapter out when, as morbid as it is, it is a big part of my story.

I first had the thought "I'm going to die" when I discovered my fear of heights. I was trying out the high ropes course at overnight camp for the first time, and I had decided to start with the log walk. I had climbed up the ladder, found my footing in the weird metal prods in the trees and made it to the wooden platform where I would take my first step and conquer the task. Except that as soon as I got up there and looked over the edge, I became paralyzed with fear. I couldn't move. My body stiffened up and I started hyperventilating. Nobody told me I would feel like this.

"I have to step onto that unstable log and walk across it? Hell no. I'm going to die up here." Literal words I screamed once I got to the top. Call me a drama queen, I dare you. For the record, if you did, I wouldn't take it personally. I've been doing theatre all of my life so there's definitely some of that in me at all times.

Drama queen tendencies aside, in that moment, I truly thought that if I took one more step that I was going to die. I stayed up there for forty five minutes, freaking the fuck out. I was terrified. Crying my eyes out and clinging onto the tree for dear life. After a shit ton of coaxing and an attempt to calm me down, the counselor who was belaying me finally convinced me to climb back down to the ground. *Look at me fancily using rock climbing terms like I know what I'm talking about...who am I kidding, I definitely googled that.*

Anyone with a fear of heights will tell you that the paralyzing fear of death that washes over you is crippling. And it's a billion times worse when it sneaks up on you because you don't realize you have have a fear of heights! It's safe to say I never got back on that log or any of the high ropes course for the remainder of my summer camp years.

The next time I thought I was going to die was the summer after graduating college when I experienced my first panic attack. A not so fun fact about panic attacks that my smart AF doctor friends have made me aware of is that a panic attack is literally described in medical school as a "feeling of impending death". So the bright side here is that at least I know my body responds the way it's supposed to when experiencing panic? Still not fucking fun, but hey, it's a win! Up until the moment of my first panic attack, I had no personal understanding of what anxiety felt like. I had been stressed sure, but nothing beyond that and, to be honest, I had spent many years wondering why people couldn't just snap out of feeling anxious. I look back now on those past perspectives of mine with love in my heart for my younger more naive self, and a deep admiration and love for anyone who has ever faced anxiety and depression in their lifetime. Until you've been through it yourself, you never really get it. You can sympathize, but you can't truly understand.

My anxiety turned on like the flip of a switch. I had never experienced it before, and all of a sudden, after having my first panic attack, it was as if I became an anxious person overnight. My only experience with anxiety this intense was when I had experienced a panic attack as a bystander. When I first met one of my best friends, she had them frequently, and I was often the person she was with when they were happening. We lived together that summer and were pretty much inseparable, so it was only natural. I had seen depression up close before

— all of the important men in my life have had depressive episodes — but this was the first time I had seen anything like this. The hyperventilating. The shaking. The sobbing. It was almost too much to bear, and this was simply as an observer.

Actually *having* a panic attack is a whole other story. It's a feeling I don't fully know how to put it into words outside of it feels like you're going to die. Like the weight of the thought or negative experience that instigated it is going to crush your chest. That your heart will smash in two and your lungs explode, all at the same time. It's fucking terrible. And the closest thing I'd ever experienced in fearing I was going to die — until my surgery.

Don't get me wrong, surgery obviously felt very different than a panic attack. Although I did have a few panic attacks leading up to my surgery that brought back that familiar feeling I had spent the last couple of years being rid of. Yay anxiety — such a fun thang to navigate, am I right?

But it was the first time in my life that my fear of dying actually felt like it could come true. Surgery isn't something to play around with. And yeah, my doctors are amazing and do this all of the time, but I've watched enough *Grey's Anatomy* to know that a simple case of the hiccups can be fatal. So an invasive surgery that could take anywhere from 4 - 6 hours? Definite death potential. Logically, I knew that the risk was incredibly low. But I'm not the type of person that can easily logic my way out of fear, so the thought that I wouldn't make it out the other side definitely took up a shit ton of space in my brain.

And I wasn't the only one. When I was in the midst of writing this book, I asked Kev what his biggest fears were leading up to my surgery. His big three were: that it would impact my mental health in a negative way, that it would change our sex life, and that I could die. Something so monumental? It doesn't just impact your life. It radically affects the lives of those around you. Something that I think so many of us can often forget.

I had gotten so wrapped up in how this could impact my life — paralyzed by all of the fears that I was facing — that for a while, I forgot to consider how this was impacting the person I love most in this world. And I'll be damned if I leave that piece out of this book. Because just as much as we go through trauma in our lives and need the tools and resources to navigate it all, **so do the people surrounding us**. They may not be directly in the thick of it, but they sure as hell are impacted by it all, and should never be left in the lurch. So here are honest AF words from the person who went through it all alongside of me, and saw the good, the bad and the ugly every step of the way — my husband, Kevan.

Amanda asked me to write a passage for this book about the fear I had of her dying around her surgery. During the surgery itself, I had those thoughts but they were fleeting. Whenever I thought it'd been too long between updates or when I watched other families in the waiting area come and go or getting their own updates about whomever it was they were so patiently waiting in those uncomfortable chairs to support.

The truth is I was much more afraid well before that. I was afraid for her life from the moment she shared with me that, despite knowing her father had the mutation—and thus she had a 50% chance of having it herself—that she wasn't ready to find out whether she too had the mutation.

I am not a person that enjoys uncertainty. In fact, Amanda tells me, frequently, that I live in a world of black and white—something I partially agree with—and the idea of this known unknown (to unfortunately quote Rumsfeld) was almost unbearable for me. I couldn't fathom how I—let alone her—could go about our lives with this guillotine hanging over us, whose rope was frayed and could drop at any moment. And, because of that, I frequently pushed her to get the test herself, to find out once and for all whether other not she had this mutation.

My fear, more so than her dying in surgery, was that one morning we'd wake up to go to a routine doctors appointment only to find out her body was being ravaged by incurable and inoperable cancer. I was afraid that I would have to watch her die, that the life we'd dreamed of would, to paraphrase this time, be nothing more than unfulfilled hopes, lost like tears in the rain. To be honest, I wasn't just afraid, I was angry.

In my mind, even though this was terrible, we were given a gift to be able to prevent cancer from taking her life. How could she have the ability physically and financially to prevent this problem and turn a blind eye to it? She was afraid of what the answer would be, I suppose, and, in the end, she was right. In my mind though, that didn't matter. Maybe I was selfish in that desire and my insistence that she get tested, I don't know. What I do know is this: I am so happy that she made the decision to get tested; to take the measures necessary to keep herself healthy now with this surgery and those to come; to ensure she stays in the world we're building together. I couldn't (and still can't) imagine what my life would be like without Amanda.

While this situation was terrible and the fear of something happening— her dying because of this mutation—will probably never totally leave the recesses of my mind. I think it has given her insight and purpose to her life (you're reading this after all) and maybe those things make all of this worth it.

Phew. That's a lot, right? It was a lot for me reading it and I lived it alongside of him. To be honest, until reading this, I didn't fully understand how much of an impact me waiting for as long as I did to get tested had on him. Just goes to show that communication in relationships isn't cut and dry or simple. *Yup, busted* — my communication wizard skills are always in practice. I'm really more like Ron instead of Hermione.

Leading up to surgery, Kev and I talked about a lot of things. But most of them centred around how I could be supported through all of it. Sure, we had conversations around his fears and I held space for him in whatever capacity I could manage amidst navigating my own mess, but the focus leading up to my double mastectomy was largely placed on me. Which, in and of itself, is a conversation for a whole other book because holy shit do our partners and loved ones need support too when we're facing traumatic shit.

Ultimately, while there isn't *really* a simple shift that can be made to help navigate this fear (and let's be honest, all of these mindset flips take intentional dedicated work to become innate practices), the biggest thing I've learned through navigating this fear of dying and hearing Kev's perspective around all of this is to **stop keeping such a terrifying fear to yourself**. Talk about it. With your partner. Your therapist. Your best friend. Your coach. Your mom. Who the fuck ever that you deeply trust and you know will hold space for you to be seen exactly as you are.

So many of the things we fear only become amplified when we keep them to ourselves because we are sure we are alone in this fear. Wrong for having these thoughts. And while the fear doesn't magically go away when we talk about it, feeling less alone and having someone else say "me too" can significantly shift the weight of it to something lighter.

So speak your **FUCK YES truths and watch the "me too"s come barreling in.** You're not alone my love.

FEAR:
MY DOG ISN'T GOING TO RECOGNIZE ME

I remember sitting down one day, a few months before my double mastectomy, crying my eyes out to Kev because I was so terrified our dog Toby wouldn't recognize me after surgery. It seemed *ridiculous*, I know, but the deep rooted fear that this surgery would change me in more ways that I could imagine was more than I could bear.

My dog is basically my child in every way. I love him as much as I imagine I'd love any human baby of my own. And while he obviously doesn't *look* like me, 'cause that would be weird, he has definitely adopted my innate goofy tendencies and my endless desire for snuggles. I love him more than almost anything in the world, and I already have to fight for his attention because he loves my husband so much...so the idea that he might not recognize me or that I'd smell different or *anything like that* had me feeling paralyzed.

After a good ol' cry and spending some quality time with my journal, I realized that my concerns really lay in the fact that I was terrified that this surgery would change my identity. And the truth is: I already had started to feel like it had. I remember a week after finding out I was positive for the BRCA gene — my husband and I were celebrating our 4 year wedding anniversary and rocking the infamous road trip up the coast from LA to San Francisco I've spoken a nauseating amount about throughout this book. *What can I say, it was a pivotal moment in my journey, okay?!* Neither of us had been before, and I had been looking forward to this trip for months, but this new found information really shifted the dynamic of the trip as I spent four out of the nine hours in the car sobbing my eyes out. I hadn't had the time to fully process what having BRCA truly meant. And I remember saying to Kev, amidst the snotty AF sobs coming out of all orifices, that my identity was suddenly this completely different thing.

    I had known myself up until that point in time as so many things — a creative, a best friend, an actor, a wife, a dog mom, a coach, a daughter, a sister, an adventure seeker, a Gryffindor*[41] — and now, all of a sudden, all I could see was a gal with BRCA. And that scared the shit out of me. One thing completely defining the entirety of who I was as a person? The idea shook me to my very core, and I felt like I was in the midst of yet another quarter life crisis.

---

[41] *I have read the Harry Potter series upwards of fifteen times in my lifetime. So when I say I identify as a Gryffindor, this is not an exaggeration. My best guy friends in college literally called me Hermione Granger for years.

There are many days when my logic brained husband drives me up the wall and all I want for him is to feel the feelings with me, ya feel me? But in that moment, he said something that really stuck with me: "This doesn't need to become your identity." At the time, this concept blew my MF mind. And it makes sense that it did! So often, when something shitty happens in our lives, we begin to interact with the world according to that one piece of ourselves and all of a sudden, our identity is entirely wrapped into that one thing…

You have a child and all of a sudden, everything you were before being a mom is left behind and your number one identifier on this planet is: Mom.

You've spent your entire life identifying as straight but all of a sudden, you meet this girl and you can't explain it but you are definitely are attracted to her in more than just a "she's really pretty" kind of way. And you question if straight is truly your identity or maybe you go down the google rabbit hole, trying to define what your new existence should be — bisexual, pan or something else?

You've spent your entire collegiate career studying to become **an engineer and playing electric guitar on the side**, when all of a sudden, your band *Mansplain* makes it big and you become a full time musician overnight*[42].

Or maybe, just maybe, **you get diagnosed with cancer** and all of the things people used to know you as — the vibrant, adventurous, travel obsessed, karaoke rockstar gal — disappear and, to them and in many ways, to yourself, you become cancer girl.

What if all of the things I'd accomplished and everything I had become up until this very point in time no longer were relevant or important because this BRCA thing swallowed it all up? Yes, I'm clearly passionate about advocating around this mission. Hell, I've written an entire book about it. But the idea of being known as one thing for the rest of my life left me reeling. I had so many layers, after all. I'm like Shrek and his onion metaphor! Layers, layers, layers! And amidst the freak out about my dog not recognizing me, I realized that this was just another example of me rejecting the idea of labels and identity in the first place.

For many people, identity is a form of pride. The labels they identify with create belonging. Community. A sense of purpose and knowing who they are. For me, labels have always felt incredibly stifling. Like if I chose to use a label, it put me into this box where everything about what it meant to be inside of said box was already decided. That it

---

[42] *I can't take full credit for this one, Kev definitely came up with the band name and I laughed out loud and couldn't not put it in the book.

was this cut and dry thing, with no room to grow. And that just wasn't going to work for me. I'd spent so much of my life conforming to boxes to fit in, even when I didn't resonate with the label *at all*.

I wore the title of **perfectionist** with pride, when all it did for me was heighten my anxiety and leave me creatively stunted.

I labeled myself as a **struggling actor,** and spent years doing just that — struggling. I hadn't for a second considered that I could be an actor and have a thriving financial life. It wasn't possible!

I took on the label of **straight** because that's all I had known. I had only been in relationships with men, but to say that I was fully straight to me meant that I had no interest or attraction to any member of the same sex, and that just wasn't true. I married a man and am incredibly happy and fulfilled, and to the external eye, that makes me a straight woman, right? To me, it's always felt more complicated than that, but I stayed inside of that label for years.

    It wasn't until I removed these labels from my vocabulary and started to own that I could create my own narrative for my life that I started to fully step into the authentic me. I stripped myself from the title of a perfectionist and owned my desire to get messy and show up, especially when I'm not feeling at all put together. I rejected the idea of continuing to struggle as an actor for the rest of my life, and started a business that has financially been able to support not just my acting career, but my life as well. I stopped identifying as straight and instead, have embraced the fact that my sexuality is fluid and that I don't need to take on a label to define who I'm attracted to.*[43]

In my opinion, labels can often be extremely limiting. Don't get me wrong, I see both sides and have found so much joy in connecting with communities that identify as one thing. All of you Harry Potter nerds, dog lovers and sevens on the enneagram are my people. But for me, labels have often felt like a set of expectations I had to uphold in order to belong — and I've never been one for fitting the mold.

My journey of being positive for the BRCA mutation has been an interesting experiment of identity for me. On the one hand, it by nature threw me into a community of womxn who were the only people in the world who could truly understand what I was going through. It's like a secret club that you never want to join, but once you're in it, you're so immensely grateful to have it. Yet, at the same time, for many moments of my journey, being BRCA positive has overwhelmingly taken over my life in ways that have felt incredibly stifling. And unlike the labels of perfectionist, struggling artist and straight — labels that felt like I had ownership and fluidity over — the BRCA gene is pretty fucking black or

---

[43] *Since writing this chapter, I've come out as bisexual and it's been the most freeing expression of myself. So I guess when the label fits, it can also be freeing. Ultimately, you do you, sistah.*

white: you either have the mutation, or you don't. There is no middle ground here. No choice to shift and take back the label in a way that felt right for me. Whether I liked it or not, I had to live with this aspect of my identity for the rest of my life. What I didn't realize at the time was that while I couldn't change the cold hard facts that I had this genetic predisposition, **I didn't have to let it define my life.**

I've spoken a lot about control in this book and I want to clear something up for a minute. I think the word gets a bad wrap. To me, having control over something means that we get to have agency over it. That we aren't just sitting ducks, allowing our lives to happen *to us*, and that we're expected to go along for the ride. I believe that there are always choices we can make that will help shape our life's path. And when adversity is placed in our path, while we may not be able to control the what, we have full agency over the how.

How we choose to react.
How we choose to feel about it.
How we let it impact our lives.

The how is the reason why two people who get dealt the same hand can experience two very different outcomes. It's why I believe that the words we use are deeply important and impactful to the life we create for ourselves. So when you're thinking about identity, remember that the words you choose to identify with are entirely up to you.

How to flip your fear of losing your identity? **Decide what you want your identity to be.** To me, this doesn't start with a label so much as a set of **values** that resonate with the root of who we are.

I spent years trying on values for size and seeing how they fit. If you'd asked me a few years back what my core values were, I would have spouted off a list of fifteen or more. What I've learned over the years is that when it comes to where we place our values, less is more. And ultimately, our gut knows best.

So let's go on a journey together, ok? Take a minute, put the book down and close your eyes. Take a deep breath in on the count of four. Hold it for four. Exhale for four. And hold for four again. Repeat this five times with your eyes closed. Ok, go. Now that you've cleared your mind, take a look at the following list of values. Without thinking about it, scan through the list and circle the ones that stand out to you. From there, I want you to choose three **Va Va Voom Values** that truly resonate with your heart.

ADVENTURE	HEALTH	PERFECTION
AMBITION	HONESTY	PERSEVERANCE
AUTHENTICITY	HUMOR	PERSUASION
AUTONOMY	IMPACT	PHILANTHROPY
BALANCE	INDEPENDENCE	PLAY
BOLDNESS	INFLUENCE	POSITIVE
BRAVERY	INNOVATION	POWER
CARING	INTEGRITY	PRECISION

COMPASSION	INTELLIGENCE	PRIDE
COMMITMENT	INTUITION	PROSPERITY
CONNECTION	JOY	RELAXATION
COURAGE	KINDNESS	RESILIENCE
CREATIVITY	LEADERSHIP	RESOURCEFULNESS
CURIOSITY	LEARNING	SECURITY
DEPENDABILITY	LISTENING	SIGNIFICANCE
DETERMINATION	LOVE	SIMPLICITY
EDUCATION	LOYALTY	SPIRITUALITY
EFFICIENCY	MASTERY	STRENGTH
ENERGY	MINDFULNESS	TOLERANCE
EXCELLENCE	MODESTY	TRANSPARENCY
FAITH	MOTIVATION	TRUST
FAMILY	OPENNESS	UNIQUENESS
FREEDOM	OPTIMISM	VARIETY
FUN	ORGANIZATION	VISION
GENEROSITY	ORIGINALITY	VULNERABILITY
GRATITUDE	PASSION	WEALTH
GROWTH	PATIENCE	WISDOM

Doing this exercise for myself completely shifted things for me. For so many years, I had felt like love, family, honesty, trust etc had to be some of my core values because that's what we're taught that we should want and need as human beings.

My three core values? Connection, courage and growth. Do love, family, honesty and trust play a role in each of these? You better believe it. But in and of itself, they no longer make the list.

Connection is at the root of everything I do. I write, speak and coach because it allows me to connect with a diverse group of people and help them feel less alone in this world. Acting is one of the deepest forms of true connection I have ever experienced — to self, to my fellow actors on stage, and to the people sitting in the audience. Connection is also at the root of everything I crave. I feel hollow without true connection in my life. My closest friends and family will tell you that a conversation with me is never superficial — hell, if we went out for coffee today, I'd immediately dig below the surface. And we'd be leaving three hours later feeling bonded on a soul level. That kind of intimacy with other people is a huge part of what keeps my love tank so damn full, and why connection is one of the deepest values in my life.

Courage is also deeply important to me. It impacts every single way that I show up in my life. Stepping into my unapologetic self took a shit ton of courage. Being honest with myself and others, going out of my comfort zone again and again, and taking steps forward before I feel ready is what living *my* fuck yes life truly feels like.

And *growth*? It's something I aspire to always be doing, in every aspect of my life. Being in a perpetual state of learning has paved the way for so much self discovery, innovation and positive shifts in my life. It's the reason I took the step into entrepreneurship in the first place. How I was able to heal from my binge eating disorder. It's the heart of why my marriage and relationships have blossomed into what they are today. I am committed to a lifetime of growth, and with it, a lifetime a self discovery.

These are my truths. My personal Va Va Voom Values. And when I took a step back and realized that my identity had nothing to do with my labels, BRCA or otherwise, but with my core values, I was able to show up for everything this new challenge put in my path with intention.

Getting clear on your values is the first and most important step to claiming your true identity. From there, you have a permanent gut check that you can keep coming back to when you have to make any challenging decision.

"Will taking this step be me showing up with my core values at the heart of it?"

Let this be your gut check to writing the story of your life. You're the author after all, my love. So don't let others put the words in. Your words are the only ones that matter.

FEAR:

I WILL NEVER BE ABLE TO HAVE KIDS

I used to believe that I was meant to be a mom. Hell, I had my entire future mapped out by the time I was twelve years old. Fall in love and get married at twenty four. Start having babies at twenty seven. I hadn't factored in the rest of the details — you know, what I wanted to do for a living, where I wanted to live, what my hobbies would be like — but I was *sure* that my path would look just like that.

And, to be honest, for a while, it looked like my life was heading that way. Legally, I actually got married before twenty four. *There go my overachieving tendencies again*! I had graduated from college the year before and was in the US on an extension of my student visa. Kev and I had moved in together right after I graduated, two and a half years into dating. I knew that he was my person. The person I wanted to spend the rest of my life with. Hell, I knew that three months into our relationship. Which surprised the shit out of me, but hey, I guess when you know, you know. And man, did I know.

By that point in my life, my future timeline that I had arbitrarily decided on when I was younger felt pretty far out of reach. I had yet to figure out how to pay the bills — getting married in a year? Having kids in 4 years? It felt laughable. But when my immigration lawyer explained our options and recommended we get married, we both dove in head first without a second's hesitation. And eleven days after my 23rd birthday, on our third dating anniversary, we got married at city hall with ring pops.

It wasn't at all how I imagined it would be growing up. The *My Best Friends Wedding* like party, huge dress and fancy AF space. It was just the two of us. At city hall. On a cold blustery day in February. And it ended up being more than I could have ever hoped for. We laughed harder together that day then I can remember. The judge who married us totally read the room and made some pretty epic jokes. And there was something so special having it be just us in the room. It was a moment I'll never forget, and the few photos we have from the day make me laugh so hard to this day because our lips are stained blue and green from the ring pops. It couldn't have been more perfect for us.

A year and a half later, we had another wedding to celebrate with our friends and family and, ironically, for that one, I *was* twenty four. And while I was and still am so sure that I wanted to spend the rest of my life with this man, getting married when I did felt early. What my twelve year old self had no concept of is how I would actually feel once I got to that age. Would I feel ready? Would I have my shit together? I was the first of my friends to get married, by a long shot, and I knew that our early to mid twenties were pivotal years of growth.

I would be lying if the fear of growing apart, or the potential of us growing to want different things didn't pop into my mind. But Kev and I were both super mature for our ages, we had worked hard to create a positive foundation based on honesty and communication, and we had already been through some really tough shit together and came out stronger on the other side. So I was confident that we would continue to build on that and grow together.

Six years later, and I'm happy to report that things are better than ever. It turns out, twelve year old Amanda wasn't so far off, on the marriage front. But kids? That's another story.

I entered into my 27th year of life feeling on top of the world, but leading up to it was, to put it lightly, a shit show. I experienced my first major what-the-fuck-is-my-life breakdown earlier than most — I had just gotten married, the second time, left to go on our mini moon to St Lucia, and came back to a full fledged quarter life crisis panic attack sob fest on my bathroom floor. I was so fucking burnt out. For the first time in years, I finally allowed myself to take a break and slow down while we were on the beach. When I came back to reality, the life that I had become so accustomed to living felt suffocating. At the time, I was working seven part time jobs, most of which I hated, and my health was at an all time low. And while I don't think you need to hit rock bottom in order to finally take a hint from the universe that things need to change (and I certainly don't recommend letting it get that far), in many ways, I'm grateful for it because it's what led me to where I am today.

That particular breakdown became one of the most pivotal moments of my life because, for the first time, I actually stopped and listened. I had known for a while that the lifestyle I had created for myself was deeply contributing to my feelings of burn out. That the negative habits I was implementing every day were a huge part of why I felt like I was perpetually struggling. But something about this time in my life felt different and finally, something inside me snapped, and I decided I couldn't pretend I was okay anymore.

So began my journey to discovering what the hell I actually wanted and who I wanted to be. I spent the next three years deep diving into the world of personal development for the first time in my life. I slowly began healing my binge eating disorder. I stopped going to the gym, a place where I'd spent two hours a day tirelessly trying to look a certain way, and started moving my body in ways that lit me up. I started journaling and asking myself questions that finally helped me peel back the layers of myself that were hiding who I truly was. I deep dove into the world of entrepreneurship and was able to not only slowly quit my soul sucking part time jobs and pay off my credit card debt, but actually find purpose in work I never imagined I would thrive at.

I was on an upward path for sure. Was I navigating road bumps along the way? Of fucking course. But overall, I felt like I was moving towards a life that was truly a reflection of my deepest desires. By the time I hit my 27th birthday, I was in a really good place. I had just gone full time as an entrepreneur and finally quit my teaching job. I had released my Live Your F*ck Yes Life podcast, a passion project of mine that I had wanted to start for years and I finally had the time and ability to do it. I had just closed a show that I loved and was gearing up to spend the next nine months working on another one that, unbeknownst to me at the time, would completely change my life for the better. My health was on an upwards swing and I felt great. I hadn't binged in over a year, my IBS and eczema had cleared up after years of struggling with it, and I felt strong and physically in shape. And all of the anxiety that had plagued me for years finally felt in control — I hadn't had a panic attack in 2 years, which, to me, was the biggest celebration of all.

I was happy. I felt on top of the world. Like nothing could bring me down. And then I found out I had the BRCA gene.

They say that there are moments in our lives that completely turn our world upside down. That alter the very trajectory of our lives.

And maybe it's a tad dramatic, but in that moment, and for many moments to come, that's what it felt like for me.

From the research I had done about the BRCA gene, I immediately knew what this meant for the future of my breasts. What I didn't anticipate were all of the other questions and decisions I needed to make around the rest of my body. A typical next step post genetic confirmation is going to see a genetic counsellor — and that's exactly what I did. I remember going into that meeting thinking I was so prepared. I had compiled a list of questions about options, specifics and beyond. I had done hours of research and knew what path I wanted to take. What I neglected to think about prior to that meeting was anything to do with my ovaries.

You see, the BRCA gene isn't just linked to breast cancer. It's certainly the highest risk from a percentage standpoint, but it also comes with significant risk of developing ovarian cancer, and a small but higher than the average population risk of pancreatic cancer and melanoma. So when the genetic counsellor started asking me questions about what I wanted to do about kids and if I had considered the IVF route or freezing my eggs, I froze. *Ha! See what I did there? Come on, it can't be all serious. You know I can't handle that shit.*

Despite being on track according to my twelve year old self's arbitrary plan for my life, at twenty seven years old, I felt nowhere near ready to have kids. Did I know I wanted them? Hell yes. I was going to be a great mom. I have a way with kids I can't explain — I always have. Maybe it's my years of babysitting and teaching, or I'm just naturally good with them, but my friends always said that if anyone was put on this earth to be a mom and raise a kid, it was me. And I agreed with them. I wanted kids. I was sure of it. Did that mean by the time I hit twenty seven I was ready for them? Hell no! But my deep down knowing that I wanted to be a mother hadn't changed…Until it did.

Having a genetic mutation complicated things in ways I hadn't anticipated. Deciding to chop off my tits was a simple albeit difficult decision. And whether I like it or not, by the time I reach thirty five years old, my ovaries or fallopian tubes, or whatever scientific advancements they make between now and then might indicate, will be removed. *Yay early onset menopause, I can't wait for that*! What I hadn't considered in all of this was the ethical dilemma I would face around having kids, and beyond that, how it would impact my feelings around having them.

The technology today astounds me. Did you know that you can have your eggs and embryos tested ahead of time for genetic mutations? I knew this was possible for a select few mutations, but hadn't considered for a second that BRCA would be included in the bunch. Turns out, it is. You can go through the IVF process, remove eggs, have them tested for the BRCA gene and choose the ones that are negative for the mutation to be fertilized and implanted. My mind was blown and I left that meeting feeling completely paralyzed with overwhelm.

I had thought about what having kids the old fashioned way could mean for us. The odds of passing the gene down were higher than I would like — 50/50. Flip a coin. And at first, I was *sure* that I would take any and every precaution to prevent my kids from having this gene and having to go through what I was going through. IVF with screening felt like the only option. But as the shock of it all wore off and I sat with all of the options, I found myself questioning more than just what path to take. I found myself wondering if I still wanted kids.

We live in a world where we are socially expected to have kids. Fall in love? Check. Get married? Check. Have a baby? It's the natural next step on the archaic predetermined escalator of life. Even twelve year old Amanda knew that. Don't get me wrong, for some people, having kids is something they know with every fibre of their being that they deeply desire. But I think for many, it's something that we never truly question because it's become so expected of us. For me, it was a little column A and a little column B, and up until this point in my life, I had no reason to question if I would be a mother or not.

Now, it's become one of the more complicated questions of my life and, honestly, one of the hardest things to navigate post surgery. I was so wrapped up in preparing for surgery and worrying about that that

I had put this topic away in the back of my mind. One thing at a time, Kev always said. And boy oh boy did I need that reminder, or else my mind would go into decision making mode for all of the things that I couldn't even begin to know the answers to. And now that I'm on the other side of surgery, it's been a major struggle.

More and more couples are choosing to go childfree, and I would be lying that right now, it's feeling like the less complicated option. I had never for a second considered a life without kids until all of this. I didn't want an army of them, but I definitely wanted at least one. And now, all paths seem complicated. We could choose to hope for the best and beat the genetic odds the good ol' fashioned way. Assuming, of course, that we can get pregnant in the first place, which is a whole other thing. But that poses an ethical and moral debate. Could I knowingly go that route and leave it up to chance? And if my future child did end up having the gene, how much guilt would I feel for being the reason they were going through it all? It's one thing to have kids before knowing you carry the gene and another to do so knowingly. Or at least, it feels that way to me.

On the other hand, I could choose to go through IVF and freeze the BRCA free embryos until I feel ready to have kids. That would remove the ethical dilemma I find myself faced with, but it opens the door to so many more questions. Do I want to intentionally put myself through IVF? While I know it has been a path for so many, I always felt that I would rather adopt then put myself through that amount of hormonal treatment if we couldn't have kids. And what about the costs attached to IVF? Plus, there's no guarantee it will even work and an even smaller chance that we will get many viable eggs without the BRCA gene.

Many of my friends post mastectomy have started taking steps down the IVF route and while some have had success, for many, it has been a struggle. One of the womxn I've met has done three separate round of treatments only to get two viable eggs that didn't have the BRCA gene. Another tried two rounds of IVF and extraction with no success only to give up and take some time off and focus on her mastectomy instead for a while before trying again. Hearing these stories caused me to pause and question what I really wanted in all of this.

Would it be worth going down a path I never really wanted to go down in the first place anyways, in hopes for a healthy baby without the gene? And then, of course, all of the questions of what my life would look like without having a child at all. Would I feel like I'd missed out on a huge part of my life? How would it impact my relationship with my friends? Who would look after me later in life when I got old and scraggly?

The ultimate truth is that there is no "right" answer. There's only what's right for me. And right now, I honestly don't know what that is — which scares the living daylights out of me because something like this feels like a fucking huge decision and knowing the answer right now would be easier so I could plan for it. *There goes my propensity for over planning again, let it be Amanda!!*

I know you can relate. Maybe not to this example, specifically, but sometimes in our lives, when it comes to something that feels like an extremely important choice, we just don't know what to do. Often this comes into play when we're trying to make a decision that would significantly alter our life's path — like ending a ten year relationship, quitting a six figure salaried position to start the Etsy shop of your dreams or up and move to the Caribbean and live on a boat for a year, where you know nobody at all. And god forbid any of those decisions have a timeline attached to it and all of a sudden the pressure is on to know exactly what you're supposed to do.

I'm still in the thick of this one. This is a situation where I don't have any answers because for me, it's a MF mess and I have moments where I think that the "right" choice for me is any one of the three options I outlined. And while many coaches, authors and experts would tell me to leave this chapter out because I can't tie it together with a neat and pretty bow, I believe that sharing the mess, especially when we're deep in it, is one of the most powerful things a person can do. What I want to offer to you instead is a permission slip to help flip the fear that my incredible therapist gifted to me around all of this: **You don't need to make this decision right now**.

I know that can feel incredibly scary, especially when you feel that there is a deadline attached to whatever you're navigating, but until you truly *know* what's right for you, it simply isn't the time. Maybe it'll take a month. A year. Maybe more. But spending all of your energy on something that you just don't have the fucking answers to is only going to create more anxiety for yourself. And I, for one, am trying to be *less* anxious, thank you very much.

Am I going to be a mom? Only time will tell. And I trust that when the time comes for me to make a decision, I will know what the right path is, for me and my family.

FEAR:
I WILL REGRET MY DECISION

Regret is an interesting beast. It's something that so many fear, and yet, for the most part, we can only truly feel it in hindsight. You make a decision that you *think* is best for you in the moment and, down the road, you realize that it wasn't the right thing. But the moment is gone. You've made your choice. You've said what you've said. And there's no going back. "The deed is done", as Lady Macbeth so poignantly states.

I've often said that I've lived my life without any regrets. That any misstep or moment I wasn't proud of led me to where I am today — a person I am deeply proud of and grateful for. So how could I regret anything that has led me here? I wore my lack of regrets as a badge of honor, as so many of us do. And it's no surprise. We've all drank the koolaid that living a life without regrets is the ultimate goal to a happy and fulfilled life. So why wouldn't we all strive to see every misstep, no matter the size or the consequence, as a moment to celebrate when, ultimately, it's what led us to who we are today.

Nowadays, I see things quite differently. I believe that it is impossible to live a life without feeling regretful. And that instead of doing everything we can to move away from it, we should have the courage to lean in and acknowledge its existence.

To get to the heart of this fear, I started with the first place we go when seeking deeper understanding: the MF dictionary. Did you think I was going to say Google? Come on, I know the world doesn't believe in paperback books and everything is moving to the internet these days, but I will always have a soft spot in my heart for the feeling of pages in a book rustling in my hands. *Plus, my eighth grade English teacher struck fear in me to always find sources in print so, the dictionary it is.*

What is the definition of regret? Regret is the emotion we experience when we think that our present situation could be better or happier if we had done something different in the past.

Sounds pretty fucking typical, am I right? I mean, I'd be shocked if to find anyone who hasn't looked back in the past and thought, "Huh, my life would be so much better if I had only done X" or "If only I'd decided to go with Y, I'd be so much happier." I know you've had those thoughts. I sure as hell have. Maybe sociopaths don't, but if you're an average human being you sure as shit have. Side note: It turns out I was onto something here — according to researcher Kathryn Schulz , "the inability to experience regret is actually one of the diagnostic characteristics of sociopaths. It's also, by the way, a characteristic of certain kinds of brain damage. So people who have damage to their orbital frontal cortex seem to be unable to feel regret in the face of even obviously very poor decisions." So, I guess, if you really want to live a life without regrets, you could lobotomize your brain. But I don't recommend it. *For real, don't be that person who goes to their doctor and tells them that I wrote in my book that getting a lobotomy was the cure to living a life of regrets. It won't end well. You've been warned.*

Okay, back to our definition. Basically, this tells us two very important things about regret. For one, it is an emotion tied to a decision that we've made. And second, a deep sense of imagination is required to conjure up a potential other path or life story that could have been created had we made another decision.

The tricky thing about regret is that it always happens in hindsight. We make a decision and, later on, once we have more information or we experience a shift in our perception of a situation, the regret trickles in. So when it comes time to making a decision in the first place, the fear of regret can be quite paralyzing. And that's exactly where I found myself when I was deciding what to do about my surgery.

Obviously, you know what I decided to do and that it was a relatively simple and quick road to my decision. I set a date for my surgery one month after finding out my test results, after all. But I'd be lying if I said that I wasn't scared I'd regret my decision down the road. What if I hated my breasts? What if I could never love the body again? What if I actually cared about breastfeeding and did decide to have a kid in the future? The what ifs majorly took over and the fear of regret took hold of my heart.

The kicker? This fear is something completely out of our control. We've demonized regret to be this awful thing that we should strive to never have to experience in our lifetime so *of course* we fear it. We aren't taught how to handle it and accept it. More on that later.

Every decision you will make in your life, big or small, is what moves you forward. I almost didn't move to Chicago when considering where to go to college. I had a boyfriend I loved back home, and had already gotten into a coveted program at a highly academic school in Toronto. Staying was the safe choice. Moving to Chicago? It was risky. I'd be going to school for a passion that would likely lead me to a challenging life financially. I'd jeopardize my relationship by moving far away. And I'd be in a city I didn't know, far from home and everything I'd known for my entire life. I had a decision to make, and I knew that either choice would drastically change the trajectory of my life.

I chose to follow my dreams and move to Chicago. My boyfriend and I eventually broke up. I fell in love with the city, and later, my Sophomore year, I met Kev. I found a family in the theatre community. It's where I met the woman who opened up the door in my brain to entrepreneurship and eventually became one of my best friends. And the list goes on and on. None of these things would have happened if I hadn't decided to move to Chicago. Would my life be equally as amazing if I had stayed? Maybe. But it certainly would look a hell of a lot different.

Were there moments when I look back and regret my decision to move? Here and now, the answer is a hundred times no. I love my life and I can't imagine it looking any differently. But throughout my journey getting here, there were definitely moments that I felt slivers of regret, even though, at the time, I was so hell bent on living a life with no regrets that I would never have openly admitted to it.

When my ex boyfriend and I decided to put our relationship on hold and leave room for exploring things with other people, I regretted my decision to move. I didn't want to break up. He was my first love — my first everything — and at the time, my best friend. I knew that if I hadn't moved, we would have still been together and, for a time, I regretted moving to Chicago because of that. *Oh, young love.* When I was super homesick, missed my friends, and got stuck with a crazy bout of food poisoning and spent the entire night throwing up MF lime tortilla chips (I still gag at the smell to this day), did I regret moving? You better fucking believe it. All I wanted was my mom. And my bed at home.

When I truly take stock of my life, I've had a shit ton of moments where I've felt regret. Some small, some big. And heading into my surgery, I knew that if I did end up regretting it, it would end up being one that would take hold of my heart for the rest of my life. And while that scared the living shit out of me, I moved forward anyways because I realized that choosing *not* to do it was also a decision. And one that, down the line, could just as well cause me deep regret. I weighed my options and I made the decision that felt best for me at the time.

When you look back on your life, can you pick out the decisions you made where you experienced regret? Maybe they happened the moment you made them. Or maybe you experienced the regret sometime afterwards. Be honest with yourself. Really give yourself a good ol' gut check. My guess is that if you truly take stock, you'll acknowledge that you have experienced a buttload of regrets in your lifetime. You probably have a list a mile long of regrets, and *I'm here to say that's okay*. Hell, it's not just okay, it's MF normal.

So far, going through with my double mastectomy is something I'm deeply proud of, and I have zero regrets about it. The moment I came to from the anesthesia post surgery, I was filled with a deep sense of relief. Relief that I was finally free of the fear that had held me back for my entire adult life. Relief that I could put this chapter behind me and move on. Relief that I was safe, supported and healthy. As I've moved through life post surgery, have I had moments that have been challenging? Negative thoughts about my body? Fears that have popped up? You better believe it. But the feeling of regret through all of this? Not once. *But that's my experience with this all.* Some womxn navigating this have moments of regret, for sure. And whether you're going through this yourself and the fear of regret is so overwhelming you don't know what to do, or you are facing something else in your life where you are feeling a deep sense of regret, please know that you are exactly where you're supposed to be.

Don't get me wrong, the feeling of regret sucks a bag of dicks. It does! It's one of the worst feelings. For me, especially so, because there's nothing to do about it and I'm a person who likes to have control over things. *What can I say, my learned perfectionist tendencies still have hold over parts of my life.* But I've learned to accept that it's a natural part of life, because with all of the science to back that up, fighting that is fucking useless.

So when it comes to flipping this fear, **I empower you to stop seeing regret as this demon thing to stay far the fuck away from, but to accept it as a part of our natural path in life.** The feeling of regret is inevitable, and so is the fear around feeling it. And we can choose to beat ourselves up about our regrets, or choose to love ourselves anyways. I choose the latter. Don't hate yourself for your missteps. Love yourself in spite of them. We're all human. We all make mistakes. If we didn't, we'd be an army of perfect Barbie and Kens and I don't know about you, but that's a world I never want to live in.

    Own your humanity. Accept your regrets. And, as Kathryn Schultz so beautifully says: "We need to learn to love the flawed, imperfect things that we create and to forgive ourselves for creating them. Regret doesn't remind us that we did badly. It reminds us that we know we can do better."

FEAR:

I'M GOING TO BE DIRT BROKE

Have you ever struggled with your mindset around money? You're in good company. I'm pretty sure I've read every book about how to shift my relationship with money, heal my money story, manifest more money, ya da ya da ya da. And for good reason: for most of my life, money has been the biggest source of anxiety for me. You'd think that with all of the body image issues, health problems, lack of purpose years and beyond that something would trump it, but the number one source for my panic attacks and years of heightened anxiety always came back to one thing: money*[44].

I grew up pretty fucking privileged. I came from an upper class home. My mom is one of the top of her field in Canada, and she worked her ass off to get there. She put herself through undergrad and her masters by teaching piano and MF made it happen as a woman in a male driven work environment. She's a total badass and one of my biggest inspirations. Largely thanks to her success and hard work, I grew

---

[44] *Yes this shit ties into my surgery big time. Patience, Iago.

up comfortably. I had opportunities that other kids my age didn't always have — I went to private school, I got to go to camp every summer, we traveled as a family. But the one thing I appreciate so much looking back is that for the longest time, I never knew how good we had it. My parents never spent money on shiny things. Our family car was an eight year old green Toyota minivan. I named her Sheila. My brother and I were expected to work for our allowance, and always encouraged to save. I literally didn't spend a dollar of anything I earned growing up and still have it in a rainy day savings fund. *Don't worry, it's been moved from my frog piggy bank.* But we certainly were never worried about where the money would come from if we needed it — my mom made sure of that. She hadn't had that kind of security as a child and was dedicated to creating a different life for her kids. So she did. And, as a result, growing up, money was the last thing on my mind.

That feeling of peace around money all changed as soon as I graduated college. I wasn't able to work through school because of my status in the United States. *Did you know that any foreigner is literally titled an alien? That title totally baffled me. I know I'm weird and all but I'm definitely no alien.* I'd come home during the summer months and teach at summer camps but other than that, my work experience was limited and I wasn't expected to fend for myself financially. As soon as I graduated and the conditions of my visa changed, I told my parents that it was time that I stood on my own two feet. I worked my butt off and found a bunch of part time jobs, and made it happen. And then the anxiety kicked in.

Becoming an adult can be a tough pill to swallow for many reasons. But, for me, the biggest of them all is the expectation that we all of a sudden are supposed to know how to fend for ourselves. Nobody teaches that shit in school. Filing my taxes? *What the actual fuck? Where do I even begin?* Building a budget and sticking to it? Creating a nest egg? Putting money away for retirement? 401ks? IRAs? *Holy shitballs my brain was exploding all over the place.* It was a rude awakening, and one that I know so many others face.

At first, the anxiety came flooding in because I was barely treading water. I was just making enough money to cover my half of a tiny one bedroom garden apartment, pay the bills and feed myself. God forbid I wanted to go out with my friends or have a date night with Kev! The paycheck to paycheck life was real and it was daunting. I found myself saying things like "I'm broke" and "I can't afford it" on the regular. And the truth is, I was, but I also stayed that way for longer than I needed to be *because of my mindset around money*.

I am, by nature, a saver. If I could, I would save every dime that I ever made and put it into some arbitrary fund for a rainy day. I've always had the deeply rooted belief that there is a limited amount of money to go around, and that I should hold onto however much I could in case I needed it down the line. *Remember that dear old froggy piggy bank where I housed every penny I ever made?* Isn't it funny how anxiety can show up around money simply by the way that we interact with it every day? The 'what if's like: "what if I'm going to need it", or "what if there's an emergency," or "what if I lose my job"? All of those what ifs are how anxiety can show up in our lives. Realizing this seriously blew my mind. It all made so much sense! Anyhow, that I-need-to-save-everything belief system stayed with me for years. And, in turn and ever so ironically, the act of actually spending money became the most anxiety inducing thing in my life. To the point where every trip to the grocery store led to a panic attack for an entire year of my life. *I wish that was an exaggeration.*

The reality of it is, we need to spend money to survive. Food, shelter, transportation — just the basics cost money. Let alone living life fully, experiencing new things, traveling to new places and having fun. Most things have a sum of money attached to them. It's the world we live in, and yet we've attached a greater meaning to it… Money can represent many things to so many different people. It can be a positive source of light. It can represent validation of a job well down. It can feel like security. Or it can be seen as unimportant, anxiety and worry inducing, a struggle. Ultimately, money is just our current form of currency. It's neither good nor bad. So why do so many of us have such strong emotional responses to money? Because of our **perception** of it.

Maybe you were raised in a family that struggled to put food on the table every night, and your constant worry around money led you to adopt a scarcity mentality. As a result, you've developed negative beliefs attached to money and feel like your life has been hard because you've lacked it. Or maybe you were raised in a wealthy family and you were given everything you could ever need. So when you look at money, you probably see prosperity and abundance, and you likely expect money to come to you with ease. Obviously these two examples are gross generalizations, and more often than not, we fall somewhere in the middle of these two extremes with our belief system, but **our relationship with money is *always* attached to our perception of it**.

While I may have grown up in an upper class home, I was always taught that money was to be saved. This planted a deeply rooted belief in me that money was limited and that every bit of it should be put away. Saving money felt intelligent and safe. Spending money felt erratic and completely irresponsible. Without realizing it, my propensity to saving as a young child had created a scarcity mindset in my adult self.

Stephen R. Covey, well known author in the personal development world, says "To change ourselves effectively, we first have to change our perceptions", and I believe that he is right. The filters we use to create our reality are incredibly biased because they are deeply influenced by our past. We've taken on the perceptions and beliefs of others (more often than not family members and partners) as our own. We see what society wants us to see instead of cultivating our own perceptions based on the thoughts we desire to create. And that's the important word here: desire. Did I like having major anxiety spells every time I took out my credit card to pay for something? Of course not. Did I want to live in a world where money felt abundant and joyful? Hell fucking yes. I simply couldn't imagine a world where that was possible. Until I started doing the inner work.

Now, I need to preface this by saying that this is not going to be a chapter teaching you the tools on how to foster an abundant mindset around money. Maybe you'll get some fairy dust sprinkled on your broke AF self that will propel you to the path of discovery for that, but there are a shit ton of books on that matter and this one isn't that. Because I sure as shit am no expert on money mindset. But I *am* an expert on mindset work and how we can shift our beliefs to reflect the reality we desire to create. That's my MF jam. And our relationship with money is a part of that.

On my path to self discovery, I realized just how messed up my relationship with money was. But I also knew how much work it would take to see a true shift take place, so I put off doing the work in that area of my life for years. I've come a long way in the last year and change — and it turns that that when you truly believe you live in an abundant world and act accordingly, your reality reflects it. My income has literally tripled in the past six months. And yes, I'm known by my support squad to often be a tad hyperbolic, but this one is straight truth. While that number and growth may seem unfathomable, it's completely and utterly unsurprising to me because of how differently I've been showing up in my life. And all of the tools I've learned throughout that journey have played a huge role in paving the way for the abundance to come forth — mayhaps that's my next book, who knows! That being said, no amount of work can save you from the deep "oh shit, how the fuck am I going to pay for this" feeling when something unexpected happens in your life.

And that's exactly how I felt when I found out how expensive this surgery would be. If I had been paying for it out of pocket, all in, at the time I'm writing this, getting a preventative double mastectomy would have cost me the better part of $110,000. *I really hope you weren't taking a sip of water when you read that because you probably spit that shit out everywhere.* The healthcare system in the United States is bat shit crazy, but that's for another time. And thankfully, because of insurance, the majority of the cost was covered. But *even so*, I'm in debt, not to mention in countless battles with my insurance company who can't seem to get the final number of what I actually owe straight. *Again, bananas. Why haven't I moved back to Canada you ask? I still don't have a good answer for you.*

But this fear? The fear of not being able to live because of not being able to afford something — anything from dinner on a random Tuesday, to rent, to a flight home for a sick parent, to crippling student debt, to MF astronomical and unexpected medical bill — is palpable and oh so fucking valid. And, as I found myself finally starting to heal from the surgery and feeling the anxieties slowly melt away, I started getting my hospital bills in the mail and I freaked out all over again.

Money is one of the leading causes of anxiety. Finances are the number one thing that couples fight about. So the fear around my hospital bills was at an all time high leading up to surgery. Luckily, I have done a shit ton of work on my mindset, especially around money, and as soon as I opened my first bill and saw a number much higher than I had been told I should expect to have to pay, I employed my very own method FUCK it method. Remember way back when in part one?

As a reminder:
F - Feel the feels
U - Uplevel your mindset and take control
C - Choose a desired feeling
K - Kick it into action

This time around, feeling the feels looked a lot like screaming "What the fuck", writing in my journal and tears coming out of my eyeballs. Was freaking the fuck out about this and feeling sorry for myself helping things? Nope. So I moved to stage two and asked myself what I could control.

I could control my reactions. I could take a deep breath and get on the phone with my insurance company to figure out how much I actually owed, even if it took multiple phone calls to do so. *If there is ever an exercise in patience, it's being on the MF phone with insurance, am I right?* I could check my savings account and see how much I'd feel comfortable dedicating to paying it off. I could look into loan options if necessary. I could figure out how many clients I needed to bring on to cover the cost and pay off the debt. As Marie Forleo says, "everything is figureoutable", and creating an action plan gave me belief that I could get through it.

I wanted to feel peace attached to all of this. I finally felt so much relief and light about the decision to have the surgery, so when something attached to it became such a stressor, I knew I had to shift my feelings around it.

So to kick the feeling of peace into action, before ever taking action attached to the money I owed, I took a deep breath, meditated and practiced an act of self care that I knew would put me into peak state — I MF worked out. *Thank you endorphins!* And I reminded myself through it all that while this felt hard and scary, what I had just gone through took a billion times more courage to face and that if I could do that, I could tackle this too.

Money is always going to be a part of your life. **You can choose to make peace with it, do your best to create abundance and live joyfully, or you can choose to allow it to be the root of all of your heartache.** It's not a sexy answer, I know, but it's the only one I know to be true. You can figure it out, my love. Think of all of the other mountains you've climbed to get here that you never thought you'd be able to face. You can, and you will. You're stronger than you know.

PART THREE:
THE AFTERMATH

WHAT HAPPENS WHEN IT'S ALL OVER?

So, you made it through whatever fucked up trauma or overwhelming AF transition you're facing. You're on the other side of it and...now what? We touched on this briefly talking about our fears, but the truth of the matter is that **this is where we so often find ourselves lost.**

The good news? You now have all of the skills you need to navigate the mess and facing your fears head on while you're going through it. *Go blast some Lizzo and throw yourself a dance party to celebrate, sistah. You've already come so far.* Now while I hate to burst your bubble, the thing that you and I both know is that facing the shit head on is just part of the human experience. What about afterwards? When, to the outside world, what you've been facing is over, but in reality, when it's all said and done, it's never really over. Days. Months. Years later. It's still fucking hard — and that's why these tools we've already covered are so damn important, and why I urge you to use them for the rest of your life, not just while you're in the thick of whatever mess you're going through.

It may feel super unsexy to hear this, but you know I'm going to tell it to you straight so here it is: your trauma is going to stay with you for the rest of your life. You can't take back what has happened. You can't reverse time, unless you've magically created some teleportation device, but we've all seen how that worked out in *Back to the Future* so... I don't recommend it. **What you *can* do is decide how you're going to show up moving forward and continue to do the work.**

Now let me preface this by saying that this is not going to happen in the snap of your fingers. I refuse to be one of those woo woo ra ra writers that puts a bow on everything and says that life is a magical ball of unicorn dust if you just believe it is so. Does the inner work make powerful shifts that can help us navigate the mess with grace, vitality and positivity? Fuck yeah it can. I've literally made an entire career learning that shit the hard way and I'm giving all of my life's work to you via this paperback goodness. *That's how much I fucking love you, okay?*

The truth is that the work never really ends because there's always shit to navigate. That being said, the more incredible tools we have in our toolbox, and people in our corner who empower us to continue to do the work and get one step ahead of the mess instead of allowing the mess to take over our lives? **That's where the magic truly lives.** Oh, and Hogwarts. Obviously.

We live in a society where we crave instant gratification. Our brains have literally become hardwired to move more and more towards things that immediately give us what we desire — why do you think Amazon is, as of 2019, the world's largest retailer. And don't get me started on the diet industry. Whole 30? Juice cleanses? Keto? We see someone magically shed 25 lbs in 30 days and we immediately hop on the MF bandwagon, only to get results that aren't sustainable and ultimately lead to more disordered eating and body shame. Been there done that. It's not pretty. While I think it's incredible yet slightly disturbing, that I can get toilet paper delivered to my door an hour after I order it if I magically run out amidst a deluge of food poisoning where things are coming out of both ends (*college Amanda had a couple moments where she could have really used that feature*), shifting ones mindset and cultivating positive coping mechanisms isn't so cut and dry.

Because, as all things in life, the ending of an especially challenging chapter of our life doesn't mean that our emotions around it magically end too. There's a reason so many therapists work on healing traumas that individuals face as children — there's a lot of shit we haven't dealt with from our past. And if it takes years of self reflection, work and intentional time to recover from something that happened twenty plus years ago, you better believe a recent trauma is going to be just as hard, if not harder, to tackle. Don't believe me? Go to therapy.

When we're in the shit of it — in my example, having and recovering from my surgery — we are handling everything head on. Doctor's appointments? I made my way there. Stripping my drains? I had Kev on standby. My post recovery strength plan? I had my workouts and physical therapy planned out for my six months post op and beyond. I was killing the U of the FUCK it method and taking control of what I could. But once I found myself on the other end of six months, after I had checked all of the boxes my doctors had given me and there wasn't really anything left to think about when it came to my surgery, I felt...lost. And my feelings of fear that I had been experiencing leading up to the main event turned into a shit ton of worry, which I truly didn't see coming.

You see, the other side of trauma? It's a dark hole of who the fuck knows what could happen, which is made a million times worse if you're already prone to anxiety. *The "what if" game is sooo fun, am I right?* The biggest thing that blew my mind is that there is *nothing* out there to support someone in my shoes post surgery. Seriously. Nobody tells you to be mentally prepared for the other side of things or how you might feel. I received all of the preparatory documents for surgery — ask these questions to your surgeons, do these exercises to help you recover quicker, get these tests done ahead of time. As for the day-of itself, I had a checklist of everything I needed to prep, what I needed to pack for the hospital and beyond. The lead up, while incredibly terrifying, was at the very least clear.

I CHOPPED OFF MY TITS

But as soon as it was over, after a few post op visits to my surgeon to make sure my healing was going well, I was expected to fend for myself. And when the worry came crashing in like a wrecking ball*[45], I was looking everywhere for some support, answers, solidarity and admission that what I was feeling was normal, and once again, I came with a big ol' bunch of nothing. So in our final section, we're deep diving into all of the things to expect *after* the mess. Because it turns out, it's messy too...

---

[45] *please tell me you imagined me circa Miley Cyrus 2017 coming in on a wrecking ball because if you did, I fucking love you*

DON'T BE A WORRY WART

I've spoken to and surveyed a lot of womxn with BRCA and breast cancer and 100% of them have expressed that they've experienced anxiety around the process leading up to surgery. Hell, you just heard a shit ton about my personal anxieties and fears, and I'm betting you can relate to a bunch of them.

But let's get one thing straight: anxiety and fear looks different on everyone — and while I'm certainly no anxiety expert, I've navigated it myself for years and the one thing I've learned to stay away from (and why I coined the FUCK it method), is *worrying*[46].

The not so simple part of the equation here? We are all so deeply wired for worry. Even when we have all the evidence in the world that everything is going to be okay, we worry! The *what ifs* take over and we create stories in our heads about what's to come...

---

[46] *worry, according to the dictionary, is a verb defined as "to give way to anxiety or unease; allow one's mind to dwell on difficulty or troubles."*

We've spent hours preparing for our final. We've rocked out the flash cards, aced the practice test and feel super confident about the material, yet **we still worry that we're going to fail.**

Our relationship is thriving. We're connecting beautifully, our communication is through the roof, we're having wonderful intimate moments together and the sex is amazing! Everything feels good, but **we worry that something is going to happen to mess it all up.**

Our business is going super well! We have incredible clients who are achieving amazing results by working with us, our income has doubled over the last quarter and we have a bunch of projects coming down the pipeline. We have no reason to believe it's all going to blow up in our faces and yet **we worry that that's exactly what's going to happen and that we'll be left homeless on the streets to fend for ourselves.**

Our partner is traveling for business. We have no reason to believe this, but **we have a gut feeling something is going to go wrong with their plane and we're freaking the fuck out.**

We're over the hump of our preventative double mastectomy, one of the scariest moments of our lives we've had to face, and **all we can think about is what if we try a position during sex and we get a little too excited, move in a certain way and an implant pops.** For the record, I told my surgeon this and he laughed in my face. I don't think he thought I was being serious — I was. Needless to say, he assured me that I never needed to be concerned about that, but still! Hello anxiety, you old friend.

Some of these examples may seem dramatic, but the truth of the matter is that worrying is a worldwide epidemic. I dare you to find me one person in your life that never worries. You can't, because it's human nature. **We worry because we care.** We care about how we're going to do on that final. We care about our relationship thriving. We care about our business that we've worked tirelessly to build. We care about the people we love surviving. And we care about our implants not exploding mid sexy times. We just do.

For some, worrying takes up a small part of our brain space. Others, especially those of us with anxiety, are chronic worriers. My anxiety tends to be triggered by life events, much like finding out I'm positive for a genetic mutation that could very well lead to my death. For a long time, I hated my anxiety, but through positive coping mechanisms, therapy and reprogramming my mindset, I've been able to make peace with my anxiety and allow it to work for me instead of against me.

In the coming chapters, we're going to walk down what anxiety and worry can feel in the aftermath of the mess, and how to navigate that piece of the mess with intention, compassion and so much

I CHOPPED OFF MY TITS

badassery. Because I know you need it as much as I do, love. Are you ready? Let's go.

WORRY:

I WON'T HAVE ANYTHING LEFT TO FIGHT FOR

It's a truly bizarre experience coming out on the other side of a major stressor or trauma. When you're going through a challenging time in your life, your body becomes accustomed to living in survival mode. What do I mean when I'm referring to survival mode? Dr. Joe Dispenza has, in my opinion, the most accessible way of describing the concept. Get nerdy with me for a second, okay? I promise you, there's a purpose.

He says: "Think of life in survival mode by picturing an animal, such as a deer contentedly grazing in the forest. Let's assume that it is in homeostasis, in perfect balance. But if it perceives some danger in the outside world — say, a predator — it's fight-or-flight nervous system gets turned on. This sympathetic nervous system is part of the autonomic nervous system, which maintains the body's automatic functions such as digestion, temperature regulation, blood-sugar levels, and the like. To prepare the animal to deal with the emergency it has detected, the body is chemically altered — the sympathetic nervous system automatically activates the adrenal glands to mobilize enormous amounts of energy. If the deer is chased by a pack of coyotes, it utilizes that energy to flee. If it is nimble enough to get away unharmed, then perhaps after 15 to 20 minutes when the threat is no longer present, the animal resumes grazing, its internal balance restored. That's short-term stress. All organisms are designed for short-term stress. We humans have the same system in place. When we perceive danger, our sympathetic nervous system is turned on, energy is mobilized, and so on, in much the same way as the deer."*47

I am deeply fascinated by neuroscience. The way our brains and our overall health are linked is, I believe, the root of healing, and I have spent more hours than I can count researching and reading all about brain health, gut health, hormonal health and beyond. The heart of this book is rooted in mindset work which directly positively impacts our mental health. So often, anxiety, stress and fear (arguably the three biggest things that can negatively impact our mental health) are viewed as separate from the body. Which is fucking ludicrous because **our brains are literally a part of our bodies**. There is so much scientific evidence to back up that what we eat, our thoughts, and the hormones coursing throughout our endocrine system (aka the thing that regulates every cell, organ and function in your body) have a direct impact on our brains and our overall mental health.

---

47 *Quote from Joe Dispenza's book, Breaking the Habit of Being Yourself

When we experience feelings of worry, fear or anxiety, our body becomes stressed. Which, from a purely body composition standpoint, creates an imbalance within our natural chemistry. Now, don't get me wrong, stress is a super natural part of the human experience. Our bodies are literally made to process stress and allow us to get back to our Fuck Yes state when we're knocked off our typical day to day path — like, for example, when you are running late for work and you spill your coffee all over your clothes two minutes before you're about to run out of the door. Stress central, am I right? And that's when your survival mode kicks in. The fight or flight response unconsciously takes over and you hustle to your closet and magically throw an outfit together so you can run out of the door without being late for work.

Survival mode is unconscious. We do it without thinking, because we're innately wired for it. Which is incredibly badass, am I right? Our bodies are so resourceful — to be able to take any stressful situation and channel our inner resources so we can react accordingly is pretty damn amazing. The thing about stress, however, is that our bodies start to break down when we spend too much time living in a stressful state. In our world today, stress is the number one cause for health issues. So stress is often perceived as a bad thing to be avoided, right? I would argue that stress inherently isn't a bad thing. The thing to note is whether it is healthy stress or unhealthy stress.

Healthy stress is an emergency reactive state for our bodies to keep us safe — like the deer's fight or flight response from above. The tricky thing is that we, as humans, have the ability to not just experience stress, but perpetuate the feelings of stress with our thoughts. So, more often than not, we live in a stressful state way longer than our bodies are made to withstand it — and that's where the chronic health issues begin. Our bodies use a lot of energy to navigate a stressful experience. So when we continue to focus on and cultivate more stress around the situation, even after the emergency state of it has passed, our body starts looking for energy in other areas (such as our vital organs, hormonal systems, digestive properties etc.) to repurpose energy to attack the issue head on. *Hello chronic illnesses, adrenal fatigue, thyroid disorders, eczema and beyond!*

I want you to think back to a time in your life where a stressful event took place and you continued to experience stress around that situation for weeks or even months afterwards. Can you recall experiencing any unexpected health issues? Maybe your acne flared up. Or you started having severe IBS for the first time in your life. Or maybe you felt perpetually exhausted and your thoughts felt fuzzy. When I was navigating life in the ten months leading up to my surgery, I had to be incredibly conscious to avoid perpetuating the stress I was feeling around it all. At times, I was able to do just that and focus on the positive. And, other times, I really struggled, and my body responded in kind. My IBS issues that I used to deal with but had gotten under control started to flare up again. Growing up and into my early twenties, I suffered from debilitating migraines and hadn't dealt with them in years and all of a sudden, I was having one a month that put me down for the count, in a dark room, feeling like I was going to die for a good twenty four hours. Not fun. And also, not surprising, considering the heightened feelings of anxiety and stress I was having.

So many womxn I've interviewed and spoken to about their experience leading up to having a double mastectomy experienced severe anxiety and mental health struggles. For some, it became so debilitating that they had to take a leave off of work. For many, they struggled through it on their own, hiding their stress and intense overwhelm from their friends and family because they wanted to appear strong. What I learned through my research and conversations with these incredible warriors? While everyone's experience varies, as we are all different humans with differing pasts and habitual coping mechanisms to show up for a traumatic event like this one, the resounding desire was to "be a fighter" through it all.

I felt the exact same way. I wanted to be a warrior woman. Embrace my inner badass and prove to myself that I could do hard things. And my double mastectomy gave me something to fight for. What I didn't realize at the time was how deeply my subconscious was living in a survival mode of stress and anxiety throughout the entire journey. And that's even with a shitload of positive coping mechanisms and habits that allowed me to show up with intention and light and joy. *It turns out that mindset coaching was the best career pivot I could have ever possibly made for myself -- thank you universe and past self!* The reality of it is that most womxn going through this process or anything traumatic in life have very few mindset tools ingrained in their day to day habits, so their version of living in survival mode ends up wrecking their emotional and mental wellbeing. And after the traumatic event is over, the aftermath of all of the damage that the perpetual state of stress has done to their bodies can be just as debilitating, if not more so, than the trauma itself.

So, what happens when we don't have anything concrete to fight for, but can't seem to get out of the perpetually stressed, overwhelmed and filled with worry state? We continue to feel like shit -- **unless we consciously choose to change our narrative.**

The good news? We can do exactly that. Our brains and bodies are incredibly adaptive. And as I mentioned above, we have the ability to change our body composition through thought and simple shifts. So, really, **it's about implementing positive coping mechanisms to rewire our bodies to move out of a stressed state, instead of continuing to perpetuate.** Now, this won't happen overnight. I know, I know, wouldn't a quick fix be fucking incredible here? *I know you know that quick fixes are a load of bullshit.* Despite the fact that we've been made to believe, and marketed to for years, that we can transform some element of our lives in 30 days, we know that it's not that fucking simple. Especially, if one wants to make sustainable changes, which I know you do. Can you make huge waves with the *right* tools in thirty days? Fuck yes you can. And that's what I'm going to share with you. A select few, simple AF tools that you can start implementing today to create sustainable shifts to get you out of survival mode and into living your fuck yes life.

Introducing...**The Fuck Yes Threesome***48

Start getting 7-8 hours of sleep every night.

Lack of sleep is the largest contributing factor to chronic stress. So start prioritizing getting enough sleep so your body is able to heal on its own.

Eat more of all the macronutrients your body needs.

This is especially for all of you emotional eaters out there, but this goes for anyone experiencing stress. Your body goes into extra stress mode when it's not getting enough nutrients. Really great news, because you can do something about it! By eating enough proteins, carbohydrates, fats and vegetables, you can start to help the stress caused my lack of nutrition to dissipate. Why? I'll tell you! And in simple AF terms, 'cause I know you didn't come here for a science lesson.

---

48 **Yeah, I went there. You knew I would. Now let's get you well fucked by these tools sistah.*

Protein gives your body essential amino acids that your body can't make on its own and it needs in order to maintain muscle, bone, hormonal and skin health. So eat that MF grass fed steak, greek yogurt bowls and your favorite smoothie to start your day with. Eat it all!

Carbs? They're your MF friend. And they are the body's key source for energy. Fun nerdy fact? When we eat carbs, and only carbs, we secrete an enzyme in our mouths called amylase. This bad boy tells your brain and body that you're full. That's why I tell my clients to stay away from the fad diets that eliminate or reduce carbohydrate consumption. You need carbs!

You wanna keep your brain healthy AF and help your body absorb all the vitamins and nutrients it needs to thrive? Eat those fats sistah! I love cooking up veggies roasted in olive oil or avocado oil, noshing on some mashed avocado with peppers and beyond. Eat those healthy fats alongside those veggies!

Establish three positive coping mechanisms to shift out of an anxious state

Think of this like your safety net to catch you when you're falling. Your immediate go-to for whenever you can feel yourself starting to spiral. Establishing positive coping mechanisms is a key way to get yourself out of long term survival mode. Why three? It sounded good. I kid, I kid -- no, for real, sometimes, you need all three! One day, you try one of them and for whatever reason, it isn't doing it for you. Or maybe you're in such a state that you need all three in tandem to flip the switch.

My three go-tos are simple AF: I set my timer on my phone for 3 minutes and I close my eyes and breathe. This intentionally slows down my nervous system and already puts me into a more mindful space. I snuggle with my dog Toby. And I put on one of my favorite tunes -- currently on blast is Lizzo's *Good as Hell* , channel my inner Beyonce and dance my ass off. This last one is especially key. Having one of your coping mechanisms linked to a physical movement is huge to shift your state of being — if dancing your ass off isn't your jam, you could rock some jumping jacks, go for a walk or even simply embody your best warrior woman superhero pose and shift your posture.

And there you have it, the Fuck Yes Threesome. The fight out of survival mode is your most important job post trauma, sistah. So take these tools and put them into action. For real, do the damn thing. Okay? Reading this alone isn't going to change your life. Take MF action.

Need the accountability? Tag me @amandakatherineloy on Instagram and let me know what you're committing to or head to www.amandakatherineloy.com/membership to take this journey to the next level.

WORRY: I'M STILL GOING TO GET CANCER.

You knew it was coming. I couldn't rock this section without including the dreaded, "what if after all of this, I still get cancer" card, now could I? You would think that getting the "you never have to see me again" from my breast surgeon would have nipped this fear in the butt, but I'd be lying if I said I wasn't filled with thoughts that I'm still going to get cancer. I had a dream just the other day that I heard those very words come out of my doctor's mouth. *Super fun dream to wake up from, am I right?* And no, I'm not talking about ovarian cancer here. That's still front and centre on my mind with my added risk. Or pancreatic cancer, skin cancer and the works.*[49] Or really any other form of cancer because, despite my diligent prevention regiment of working out, positive mental health coping mechanisms and nutritional supplements, anything is possible.

I mean that even after going through all of this, there's a teeny tiny worry in the back of my mind that I'm still going to wake up one

---

[49] *remember how I mentioned that having the BRCA gene mutation means having a higher risk of not just breast cancer, but ovarian, pancreatic, prostate and even melanoma? Yeah, it's super fun.

day, take a shower, find a lump and find out that I have breast cancer. Does it make any logical sense? Hell no. Having my preventative surgery reduced my risk by up to 97%, so my odds are pretty fucking good. Hell, the odds that *anyone* even without the BRCA could develop breast cancer in their life is 1 in 8. Isn't that statistic crazy? On average, one in eight womxn are at risk of developing breast cancer in their lifetime. That's a hell of a lot bigger than my 3% risk. And yet that worry? It's still there and I'm not sure that it will ever go away.

Perhaps it's because it's been so deeply rooted in me for as long as I can remember. Maybe it's because I tend to view life through a feeling based lens instead of a logic based one — something Kev and I have navigated in our relationship for years.*[50] Or maybe it's because, while extremely rare, I know a handful of womxn who have stories just like mine, went through with their double mastectomy and then still ended up getting diagnosed with breast cancer. *Yeah, sit with that for a minute. It fucking sucks.* I know the likelihood of this happening to me is incredibly low. My post surgery pathology results came back cancer free, and that's generally where the discovery takes place, but still, it's scary. And I think a small part of me will always worry about it.

---

[50] **Totally understand that it's not always the case, but I always find it so fascinating how many cis gendered, heteronormative relationships have a similar dynamic between the male and female partner.*

Maybe there's something in your life you constantly worry about coming back to haunt you. An old addiction that took years away from you and you worry about the possibility of going back down the addiction spiral. *While you know you haven't had a binge in over three years, you spent so many years binge eating that it's always in the back of your mind.* An ex who even though you know isn't good for you, you know you'd have a super hard time turning down if they said they wanted you back. *The heart wants what the heart wants sometimes, even when it doesn't make any fucking sense.* A stupid AF decision you made when you were younger that could made it hard for you to get the job of your dreams. *You go after it anyways, in hopes it doesn't slow you down.* Or maybe, just maybe, you are just like me and the worry of the C word coming back to haunt you is so fucking real it can be debilitating at times.

The truth? All of those worries are and have been mine. And yeah, for a while, they took over the landscape of my mind. Until I started looking at the event itself as a gift instead of a life sentence.

You see, the worry around these things can lead to some serious pain. Our hearts feel heavy. It can cause us to sink into depressive episodes and we can get stuck in victim mode super easily if we aren't careful. If there's one thing I know, it's that I refuse to be a victim of my story. I want to choose to show up every day as the version of myself that is living her fuck yes life — and that gal? She learns from her mistakes. She stands unapologetically in her truth, even when the truth is hard to swallow. She accepts her worry wart self, but doesn't allow the what ifs in her head to stand in her way of taking action. And above everything, **she chooses to look at everything she faces as happening *for her* instead of *to her*.**

And you can too. My goal for you at the end of reading this book is to have a set of tools for your toolbox to be able to use in your own life to help you cultivate *your* fuck yes life. You already have so many to pick and choose from, but this one? It's one of my favorites. I've been implementing these words into my own life for years now and it's been huge for me.

When you're facing a worry around something of this weight, say this affirmation out loud and embody the feeling around it:

"The situation is neither good nor bad, it simply is."

Let's try it together now. Find a comfortable spot. Close your eyes and take a deep breath in on the count of four. Hold it for a count of four. Exhale for another count of four, and let it sit for a count of four. Repeat four times through and then speak these words aloud with conviction three times in a row.

Sit in the feeling of what it would mean to actually feel this way. That the worry you're experiencing simply is — it's not good or bad. The truth of the matter is that you are not going to immediately snap your fingers and actually believe these words. That's why so many people think affirmations are a load of bullshit. The reprogramming takes time, but when we do the work to embody the words and feelings we desire, often starting with affirmations such as this one, we start to make progress towards feeling less overwhelmed around all of the worries in your head.

Worrying is so often viewed as a negative thing, and yeah, the feelings around it can suck, but they don't have to. That's where the power of mindset work comes into play and why I love this affirmation so fucking much. It serves as a beautiful reminder that all feelings are worthy and that worrying doesn't have to feel like shit when we see it as a part of our natural makeup.

WORRY:

WHAT ARE OTHER PEOPLE GOING TO THINK?

Do you often find yourself wondering what other people are going to think about something you do or say? Or how they'll feel about who you are as a human being? It's human nature to want to be liked. Hell, to want to be loved so fiercely for every piece of who you are. To be seen and appreciated. And if you're anything like me, I'm guessing you struggle a lot when people perceive you as something other than what you truly are.

I have a lot of things I struggle with — 'cause I'm MF human. I hope this book thus far has proven to you that despite all of my success, I am a normal twenty something year old gal who most definitely does not always have my shit together. I'm figuring it out as I go. Taking what works, trying shit that doesn't, sometimes taking unintentional detours away from living my fuck yes life, all the while being endlessly committed to doing the work and implementing the habits to get one step closer to my baddest, most epic self. Through all of the mess, the biggest thing that I have struggled with, and continue to navigate in my own life today, is how I react to what other people are saying about me, or what other people think about my life and the decisions around it.

I would love to sit here and scream to the universe that I don't give a fuck about what other people think. But that would be a bold faced lie. I've heard so many other prominent people in the self development world claim that other people's opinions don't impact them, and while I deeply hope that that is true for them and that they are so high vibe and self actualized that no negative comment can get to them, as a human being and someone who teaches mindset work for a living, I call bullshit.

Maybe I am not on their level yet. *Maybe I never want to be.* But I would bet you all of the sushi rolls and seaweed salad on the planet (which, for the record, is absolutely the way to my heart) that while I'm sure that they have so much clarity around who they are as a person and the work that they do on the planet, the haters and the trolls get to them too. And when they're perceived as something other than what they are intending to put into the world, it hurts. And I know it hurts you too. So from one transparent gal to another, know that I see you and that you are not alone.

For all of my adult life, I have desperately wanted people to like me. To see and understand me for who I am at my very core. I was first aware of this desire when I moved to Chicago for college. I was all of a sudden jumping into an entire new pool of people I had never met, and I was desperate to be liked, accepted and seen for my goofy, vivacious and at times suffocatingly loving self. For a lot of my young adult life, I thought that the path to this acceptance was fitting in — listening to the same music that everyone else jammed out to, wearing the same Forever 21 clothes everyone wore, looking a certain way so I didn't stick out, the works. I see so many womxn today navigating similar things. It's no wonder the diet and retail industries capitalize on marketing towards the insecurities of womxn. It worked on me, that's for damn sure. Sure, wearing the "right" clothes and losing "enough weight" to look a certain way can seem like a shiny way to be accepted and seen, but the reality of it is, it's just another step causing you to move further away from who you truly are. Which fucking sucks a giant bag of dicks because it leads to a need for a shit ton of mindset reprogramming later on in life that most people never invest their time and money in pursuing. *Obviously not you, you smart cookie. You're reading this goddamn book. You're killing the game. Keep it up.*

I think that the real struggle we have around perception lies in what other people think about who we truly are. Our insides. The things that make us tick. Our personality. The essence of our hearts, our desires, and the things that light us up. Sure, the surface things can be a shiny penny to create a mask to the outside world to protect our hearts — but what about when we share our most vulnerable thoughts, feelings and most authentic version of ourselves to someone or someones and we get rejected? That shit hurts like a giant pile of garbage on fire being catapulted at our heart. A dumpster fire, you might say. *You're welcome for that imagery and the bachelor nation reference.* And that's where the true pain around perception lies.

Hear me out — I know some of you are probably thinking that the real struggle here lies in the perceptions people have around quick snap judgements that are made when looking from the outside in. And there's certainly weight to that. I am a part of a heteronormative seeming marriage, and yet I identify as a bisexual cis gendered female. When people see me walking down the street, holding hands with my husband, do they assume I'm straight? You better believe they do. Assumptions of this nature can be frustrating, and I understand that frustration. But the heart of this issue and this deep ingrained worry lies elsewhere.

In all of my years working with womxn navigating low self worth, paired with my own deeply rooted struggle around the topic, I've seen a pattern come up time and time again. As human beings, we don't simply want to be liked; *we have a deep need to be loved for who we really are.* And yet, we're so fucking terrified to show our true selves to the people and the world around us that we play small. We put our energy into dimming ourselves down to fit into a prescriptive box that society and history has told us is where we will be the safest. And we struggle to let our true, unapologetic selves shine through.

I did that, for years. And every single client I've ever worked with has done the same in some capacity. Why? At the core of it, I believe it's because **we're so worried that if and when we vulnerably share who we truly are at our core, we won't be loved and accepted**. And that feeling of not being seen and deeply loved for all of ourselves is so unbearable to consider. So we shield ourselves from facing that kind of rejection because it's the best way to protect our hearts.

Feel familiar? This was the biggest lightbulb moment of my life. And this realization is what has allowed me to start taking the steps to be less afraid about speaking out about the things I believe in and showing the vulnerable, not so sexy parts of myself to the people I love most and to my Live Your F*ck Yes lifers — all of you book readers, podcast listeners, social media followers, community members, clients and beyond.

My journey with BRCA and navigating my surgery threw an interesting curve in my personal work around the concept of perception. For the first time in my life, I truly didn't care what other people thought. I was so relieved to be taking action for my health and advocating for myself, and I was incredibly passionate about being a voice for all of the other womxn going through the same thing I was. I was also furious that the public representation and information around BRCA in young womxn was so fucking small, so my anger and my drive to change that outweighed my own insecurities for the process leading up to surgery. I'm still equally as dedicated to the cause and being an honest advocate for BRCA, but the nagging voice in my head that, as you've seen, I so lovingly have dubbed Jeanine*[51] started coming out in full force saying:

"What are people going to think about this decision?"
"How can I call myself a wellness coach when I have something that's not real in my body?"
"My trauma was less invasive and challenging as hers. Are other womxn in the community going to think my story is less valid and important?"

I told you, Jeanine can be a bitch sometimes. But she can also sometimes be right. The truth is, I'm sure that every single person I know or that is in my community has had a perception shift about me through all of this. You included! And I don't mean that as a negative thing — you've read about me navigating this journey and looked at me in a new light, according to your own perspectives and the way that you see the world. Maybe you now see me as a strong as hell badass who made a decision to tackle her fears and dove into the deep end. Or maybe, you are reading this and are thinking that I'm a total fraud and should have never written a book around the subject. Or anything in between! I couldn't possibly know what you're thinking because I'm not in your head.

---

[51] *pro tip: name your inner voice. It's way more fucking fun.

And the same goes for you, love. I know how scary your head can be. You're sitting around after the mess and freaking out about how other people are going to look at you now and the words your inner shit talker is telling you — you know, the shitty comments your head has made up that other people are inevitably making about you? They suck. There's no sugar coating that piece of the puzzle here. But what I do know is that while these thoughts buzzing around our brains can feel debilitating, ultimately, those words have nothing to do with what other people are thinking.

Wanna know why? **Because those words are your thoughts. Not theirs.** You see, perception is a tricky thing. We worry about it so deeply, and yet we have absolutely no control over it whatsoever. Sure, we can attempt to alter people's perceptions in small ways, like rocking that super cool romper that is totally out of our comfort zone and we think makes us look fresh AF, but we have absolutely no idea about the opinions that choice will cause others to make about us. The gal you randomly walk down the street next to, who also happens to be a super bubbly and outgoing person, might look at you in your epic romper and think, "Damn, she's super stylish and wearing such a bright color. She must have such a vivacious and fun personality!" While the gal on the bus who is super tall and always struggles to find rompers that actually fit her frame might look at you and think, "Booo — you romper wearing but probably very nice person — stop trying so hard to fit in."

I know, I know, a silly example to make a super fucking important point: when someone doesn't like you or agree with something you're doing, it's because they are looking at you through their own personal lens of how they view the world. **It has nothing to do with you, and everything to do about them.** And that's how we begin our mindset reframe around a worry that is so rooted in each and every single one of us.

Don't take stock in what your inner shit talker is claiming other people are feeling and saying about you. Or hell, even what people are *actually* saying about you. 'Cause let me tell ya, it wasn't all Jeanine doing the talking for me. Sharing about this journey online (or anything around a sensitive or stigma based subject) is always going to bring a concoction of responses and perceptions. I had my fair share of it all, and I know you have too. **The key here is remembering that what matters most at the end of the day, is how you view yourself.** The only lens that matters here is your own. You have to live with your choices, your actions and your reactions. That's on you. Other people's beliefs and perceptions? It says nothing about you, and everything about *their* beliefs, *their* struggles, *their* traumas, and the work that they need to do on their own healing journey.

So the next time you start to worry about what other people think, turn on your **Fuck Yes Glasses lense** and **remember that their perception speaks volumes about who *they* are and where *they* need to do the work, and nothing about your worth.**

WORRY:
SHE'S DOING SO MUCH BETTER THAN I AM

You know I couldn't write a book without digging into the comparonitis game we play with one another. It can get fucking vicious, especially between those of us who identify as female. Don't deny it, sister. I know you've compared yourself to other womxn before. We all do! It's MF human nature, especially in our day and age where we have access to the lives of other people at the touch of our fingertips.

I believe that, at the root of it, we struggle with the comparison game out of a **worry that what she has or how she's doing in life is somehow indicative that what we have, how we're doing or who we are isn't good enough.** Now, don't worry, this isn't going to be a chapter where I end by compelling you to use the mantra "I am enough" and plastering it everywhere in your wall, your bathroom mirror and chanting it at the top of your lungs as a part of your morning routine. As wonderful as the intention behind doing so may be, it doesn't work. At least, it didn't for me. I've tried it. And it didn't fucking change the way I felt about myself for a second. It just made me feel like I was lying to myself because while I was saying the words *I am good enough*, I continued to believe that I wasn't.

I'm guessing you've struggled with the same in some capacity. Not feeling pretty enough, smart enough, successful enough etc. And, nowadays, these feelings have only amplified as we see other people, who, from the outside looking in, are just like us and seem like they have their shit together. Hint: they don't. They just do a better job at hiding their mess. Or maybe, they're a few steps further along in their journey so comparing your now to their now is so deeply unfair to your heart. This is why I've made it my mission in life to share the mess and be transparent AF in everything that I do. The curated feeds on Instagram and the highlight reels are 90% of what we see online, and early on in my journey, it really fucked me up.

I created my first Instagram account in 2012 as a way to document my new health & fitness journey. I joined a program that I thought was going to finally get me in shape and help me lose the 30 lbs of weight I'd gained freshman and sophomore year of college. The founders of the program were really using the growing popularity of social media platforms to their advantage (which makes complete sense!) and encouraged all of the people participating to create an Instagram account to hold themselves accountable. At the time, I was desperate for a change. And the little kid inside of me that just wanted to fit in and not be bullied for her size was finally ready to make a shift, so this seemed to be the thing I had been looking for! I mean, the womxn who founded the program were fit AF and looked like mermaids. The other womxn who had done the program to a tee got results, so why couldn't I, right? I could look like a MF mermaid too. Or, at least, that's what went through my mind. Looking back and a shit ton of therapy and self discovery later, I now recognize this moment as the beginning of my four year battle with orthorexia, binge eating and serious body image issues.

Sound familiar? Every woman I've met has, at some point in their life, struggled with their body, fitness or food. And the internet can often perpetuate that struggle. Now, I don't believe that there's anything inherently wrong with getting accountability online for your health goals. Obviously! I help other womxn do just that in a super fucking incredible and intentional way with my Live Your FYES Wellness Corner and with my one on one clients. And I certainly think it's awesome to follow the journeys of people online that truly inspire you, share your values and empower you to love yourself for who you are. However, the decision to start this account in the way that I did ended up being incredibly detrimental to my long term health.

For one, the type of fitness routine and nutrition plan that was being recommended to me through this program was, unbeknownst to me at the time, *not healthy*. It perpetuated diet culture to a tee. I was being told to do slim downs consistently where I didn't eat carbohydrates (or really anything beyond lean protein and vegetables), I wasn't supposed to consume more than 1200 calories a day, any sort of treat was "off limits", and I was expected to run for 30 minutes every morning and do a strength training routine in the afternoon. Nodding your head in mutual understanding and frustration? The diet culture trap has gotten so many of us it makes me sick. And it sucks because we simply didn't know any better. Maybe you did Weight Watchers. Or rocked the cabbage soup diet. Or got roped into a year long CrossFit package and into the bodybuilding world. Most of the womxn I have ever spoken to have gone through something similar and it's fucked them up royally for years. And that's exactly what happened to me. I wasn't eating enough nutrients a day with what the plan I was following called for, which led to my binge eating disorder. When your body is literally screaming at you to eat something, it's no wonder you MF raid the pantry and eat whatever you can get your hands on. In my case, it was usually huge sleeves of Oreos, ice cream, tortilla chips and salsa or MF Nutella out of the jar. My binge monster, as I liked to call her, came out strong in the form of intense sugar cravings that had to be satiated ASAP. It was overwhelming AF and I now know after years of learning about how our body functions, nutrition, womxn's hormonal cycles and beyond just how much damage I did to my body.

I'm grateful for the experience of it all because it was 100% the precipice that led to my giant quarter life crisis breakdown out of which bloomed my step into entrepreneurship. But it still fucking sucked and I would not wish my health struggles on anyone. Not even my crazy downstairs neighbors who ask if I'm a burglar ever time they see me. Literally. Every. Time. *You would have thought that may have stopped four years into living there but nope. We're still here.*

The second reason this was not positive for my long term health is because it amplified the already inherent cycle of comparison going on in my life to an insane level. I'm a competitive person by nature. Seriously, beat me at any board game (you *probably won't 'cause I'm awesome*), and you'll see that side of me come out. And at twenty two years old, when I started this program, I was not only dealing with my inherent competitive nature, but also the peak time of my life when I was experiencing all of the insecurity. I would spend hours scrolling through these other womxn's profiles who were doing the program too and could only feel good about myself when I started seeing results like theirs. She had abs? I wanted them. She made this salad? I needed to make it too. And don't get me started about the Instagrams of the trainers. Picture perfect curated content where all that was shown as beautiful and fit were size two tanned womxn with a thigh gap, abs for days and long mermaid hair. Something I could never relate to and even at the peak of my orthorexia days when I could fit into size two clothes, I could never look like.

Now let me be clear — I'm not hating on the way they looked. I simply couldn't see myself in them. And there was no representation of anyone that looked like me as "success stories" in any of their promotional materials. So while, at the time, I believed that following their program and them would be inspirational, it ended up being incredibly harmful for what I needed at the time (and honestly, what I continue to need today).

I stopped participating in that program years ago — after more years than I'd like to admit doing it — because I could see that I was tired of trying so hard to be like someone else and **I hadn't gotten any closer to loving me**. And years later, coming out of my double mastectomy, I found myself faced with the comparisonitis game all over again. And I wasn't alone.

"How was she able to do pushups post surgery so quickly?"

"Why do her breasts look perfect and mine look so weird?"

"She's doing so well after surgery. She's being present for her kids, is back to normal life after a week and I'm over here three weeks post op and can barely get out of bed, let alone be a good mom to my kiddos."

...And that's just the tip of the iceberg of some of the things I heard from other womxn post surgery who spent their days comparing themselves to other womxn they were connected with on Instagram who had also had the same (or similar) procedure.

Sharing my journey online was a decision I wrestled with for a long time. I knew that there would be womxn who would compare their experiences to mine — it's an inevitability of sharing your life online — and I wanted to be a source of inspiration and education. Ultimately, I decided to share my recovery process in pretty great detail for the very same reason that I wrote this book; there is so little information on what this process actually looks like and *feels* like and my fiery heart couldn't let that shit fly anymore. And because of deciding to do just that, in the past year alone, I've connected with thousands of womxn, online and in person, who have BRCA, breast cancer and beyond. And every single one of them had a different experience than mine. Were some aspects similar? Fuck yeah! But what once would have been the comparisonitis game quickly turned into a giant **awe-fest of badassery**.

Instead of hearing their stories and seeing where my experience lacked, I honored my journey as my own and celebrated them for theirs. Instead of looking at others online and assuming that every shiny empowering photo of them post surgery was the whole truth, I reminded myself that most people don't share the whole story online because it's vulnerable AF and scary to do so, and that what I was seeing was a small part of the entire picture of their journey. And, above all, I celebrated my personal wins. The things going well in my life. That I was excited about and proud of.

Could I have gone down the comparisonitis game and proceeded to make myself feel like shit? Le duh. And sometimes, I did. 'Cause hey there, I'm human just like you. *Unless you're really a wizard, in which case, where the fuck did my Hogwarts letter go, Dumbledore?* But in the end, I always came back to my decision to see life through a celebratory lens and employ my **awe-fest of badassery**. Because someone else's success does not equal my failure. And spending hours at a time focusing on how much better they have it than I do isn't doing anything for me but making me more miserable. And that's the key to flipping the script here and taking the comparisonitis out and the badassery and celebratory of self in: once again, the power of perspective.

Your journey is uniquely yours, and when you can choose to accept and love yourself for where you're at and move yourself to make choices that allow you to take steps towards your most empowered self? That, my friend, is where the real magic lies.

WORRY: MY SCARS MEAN I'M BROKEN

Scars are an interesting thing. We all have them in some small way — an old cut that was deep enough to leave a mark, a birthmark or mole removal, the remnants of the c-section you had to bring your little into the world or maybe, just maybe, a leftover reminder of a traumatic event. Scars always tell a story. Physically, they can often be intense reminders of pain. They certainly have been for me.

Like that time I was playing ballerina with my brother in the middle of our living room and he got so dizzy from spinning that he spun head first right into the corner of our piano bench and needed three stitches in his forehead. Every time I see that scar on his face, I'm reminded of the fear in my brothers eyes and the guilt I had that as his older sister, my idea of fun put him in harm's way.

Or the scar on my back that looks like a fossil. You know when you're in those get to know you circles and someone always asks to know a fun fact about yourself? That's always my go to. But the truth is, it's not so fun. I often resort to humour when I'm uncomfortable. *I'm guessing you figured that out by chapter two. You smart brilliant AF human, you.* The scar on my back has been a source of pain for me ever since I got it. I was born with a birthmark on my back. Smack dab in the spot where you'd see a tramp stamp. Damn birthmark getting in my way of my tattoo dreams! I don't remember the details around how or why we discovered this, but when I was eight years old, I had to have it removed because the doctors told my mom that it was precancerous. It was supposed to be a super simple procedure — the doctors were to numb my back and essentially scrape it off. Well, that's what they were supposed to do — but instead of cautiously scraping it off as intended, they actually dug it out. This was my first major medical procedure growing up and, as a kid who absolutely hated anything to do with doctors or needles, it was super traumatic for me. I can still remember the face of the doctor who did it. The smell of the room. The feeling of the needle going into my back to numb the area. My mom's hand squeezing tight around me so hard it felt like my hand might explode. It was done twenty minutes and eight stitches later.

As a kid, the thought of how having a scar might impact me hadn't even begun to cross my mind. And at first, as soon as it healed, outside of the fact that I thought it looked like the fossil I had found on my excavation trip to the Badlands in Alberta, Canada the year beforehand, I didn't pay it much mind. But a year later, when I started going through the beginning stages of pre teen hell and self loathing, all of that started to change.

Scars are tricky. While they literally represent a reminder of a physically traumatic experience to our bodies, emotionally, they often represent a shit ton more than that. My fossil scar was the first time I experienced the emotional side of things when it came to any sort of physical trauma. Growing up, to me, my scar was a constant reminder that my body wasn't perfect. That I could never look like the other girls in my class, in the movies, or in magazines because I would always have this scar. I would look at it in the mirror and be disgusted. And that feeling around it went on well into my twenties, especially at the height of my struggle with body image, orthorexia and my binge eating disorder. The only thing that helped was that it was on my back so unless I turned around while looking in the mirror, I couldn't see it.

With all of the work I've done on loving myself from the inside out, I don't much think about my fossil scar anymore. Truth be told, I've come to love it as something that makes me uniquely special and badass. I mean, who else can say that they have a scar on their body that looks like a fossil? *If you know someone, send them my way. We'll start a club.* But the idea of being able to accept my new breasts and the scars that would inevitably come with them was a daunting task for my brain to compute and let's just say that as soon as the meds wore off and I took off the sexy as all hell compression bras that had been keeping the swelling down and saw my tits for the first time, the worry train began to take its toll.

There was obviously a part of me that was worried about the physical aspect of things, as I deep dove into all of my fears around that in the Frankentits chapter. As you discovered, for me, it was ultimately less about the actual physical changes on my body, and more about how terrified I was about how they would impact the way I felt about myself. And I had good reason to feel this way. Basically every womxn who I'd spoken to who had had a double mastectomy also really struggled with learning to love their scars and their post surgery body. So, to me, it felt like an inevitable experience.

Coming out of surgery and heading back into "normal life", I remember feeling about my scars on my breasts the same way I felt about my fossil scar growing up. I immediately went back into the same mindset ten year old Amanda felt: "how can I make this go away so I can feel beautiful again?" I had gotten a few recommendations for scar cream reducers and had bought them all*[52]. I was ready to go and determined to make the marks left by my incisions at the very least fade. But, in the end, I only used it for a month post op before I stopped altogether.

For longer than I would like to admit, I was so worried about my scars being a reminder that I was broken that I forgot about all of the tools that I preach and teach. It amazes me how much the way we look

---

[52] *Truth: I only ended up trying two of them and only liked one because it was actually natural and while the point of this chapter is not about finding ways to reduce your physical scars, if that's something you want to do for you, no fucking judgement here sistah! I personally loved the boobie butter brand.

can so deeply dictate the way we feel about ourselves. As you know, I have felt this in my own life, and I see it day after day with the womxn I work with as a coach. Sometimes, and by sometimes I mean more often than not, the teacher needs the lesson just as much as their students. And holy shit was this the case for me around this entire experience. I was so laser focused on the scars themselves instead of what the root of the worry was — that seeing my scars every day would be this awful reminder to myself and to others around me that I am broken. And this is where the real healing begins, **and the deep work truly lies in how to go from feeling broken to feeling whole.** This might sound and feel like an impossible task for you. I get it, it did for me too. But trust me on this one, okay? The bread and butter of this is where we place our worthy-ness — in the external or the internal.

We are all hardwired, largely thanks to societal norms, to attach our worthy-ness to external factors.

What do I mean by this? Examples of external things could include: the number on the scale, whether or not you are married, the amount of money you make, the job you have, the size of the clothing you wear, and, you guessed it, how your body look. I've heard this phenomenon described as shiny penny syndrome by many in the self development world, and while I like the imagery attached to it, I'll do you one better. Every time I think about this concept, all I can do is picture the scene in *Finding Nemo* where the seagulls are going crazy screaming

"Mine! Mine!" when they see Nemo on the ground. Can you picture it? *53

For our sake, let's call it **The Seagull Syndrome**. It's way more more memorable and way more hilarious, which is how we do things around these parts. The Seagull Syndrome is what putting our worth in external factors feels like to me. We want something so badly and we think that once we get it, we'll feel full. Satiated. Content. When in reality, it's not that cut and dry. Those seagulls? Sure they might feel content for a moment once they actually get what they desire, but a minute later they're hungry again and looking for the next fish to swoop down and the cycle begins anew.

Think of a moment in your life when you have gone after something that you actually achieved that fits into The Seagull Syndrome category. Maybe it was those jeans that had been sitting in the back of your closet for years that you desperately wanted to fit into so you could "get your body back". Or the dream partner you manifested who you believed would complete you. Or the $10k month in your business that you so desperately wanted so you could feel like a "legitimate entrepreneur".

---

53 *If you haven't seen it, I don't know what to do with you. It's a MF classic and Dory is basically my soul sistah. Go watch the movie and come back to me, ya fucker. You're welcome in advance.*

Let me guess — you got it and you celebrated for a moment. Maybe even a few months. And then before long, the unworthy feelings set in again. I've seen first hand with all the womxn I work with and from my own personal experience that this happens not because achieving those things make us inherently less worthy/beautiful/pick your poison, but because we spend so much time going after The Seagull Syndrome experience and external validation and so little time doing the inner work to genuinely love ourselves.

That's why the internal work is so fucking important. Because until you truly can be content with who you are are the inside, the external shit isn't going to matter. Hell, it could even be a serious detriment to the way you view yourself. Like my scars, for example. When you find yourself looking for your worthiness from the outside in (hell, you're probably doing it right now in some aspect of your life because we all fucking do it), think of this chapter and remind yourself that nothing, I repeat **nothing**, outside of yourself will ever be able to provide you with the feelings of worthiness and wholeness you're craving. The potential for those feelings? **They already exist inside of you.**

The trick here to get you started on this journey? You guessed it. MF flip your perspective. When we focus on the things we don't like about ourselves, and we live in the pain of the past, we only amplify the feelings of suffering. That's why gratitude is so fucking powerful. I know, I know, you've heard it a million times before and there's a reason for that. So if you haven't been writing down 3 things a day you're grateful for, why the hell not?!? I resisted that shit too, out of pride. "I'm too good for that gratitude shit!" Nope, I'm not. I fucking need it. And you do too.

Gratitude literally helps brings our awareness back to the now. To what is, instead of what we are lacking. Which is hard AF to do on our own because our brains are so hardwired to focus on what is royally sucking. So if there's a tool that literally helps shift the chemistry of your brain to do just that, why the hell wouldn't you do the damn thing...is what I asked myself. Maybe you're asking it too. So just fucking do it, as Nike should say.

Got it? Good. After you write down 3 things in your life you're grateful for every morning, I'm going to add an even more expansive tool to your toolbox. Y'all ready for this?*[54] I give to you: **future gratitudes.**

How it works? Every day, you're going to think about something you desire. Maybe it's a feeling you want to cultivate more in your life. Or maybe it's even a MF Seagull Syndrome object or milestone in your life that would feel really damn good. The key is to connect it to how you want to feel. Remember the C of the FUCK it method? Core

---

[54] *If you didn't just break out into "Ya'll Ready For This" we may have to reevaluate our bestie status.*

desired feelings? This is key here too! Not sure where to start? Here are some examples from my own life to give you an idea.

"I am so grateful for my ease-filled work for myself job that allows me to express my creative self and make a MF impact on others in an intentional and substantial way. I feel so fucking empowered every time I get to put on my work hat and I'm grateful as hell for that."

"I am so grateful that I had the courage to invest in a coach. I am finally seeing the changes I've been so desperately seeking. I can see a light at the end of the tunnel for the first time in years, and I am so proud of myself for doing the work to help me heal."

"I am so grateful for the strength and the relief this experience has given me. My scars have become such beautiful reminders of my badassery and strength and it has allowed me to connect with some of the most incredible soul sistah womxn who have become like sisters."

These have all been future gratitudes of mine before I had achieved the moment and the feelings around them. And each and every single one of them I have cultivated in my life by putting my energy towards those desires and feelings. Where you put your focus in your life is where your life expands. Truly. So put your energy there sistah and rock your future gratitudes. And before too long, you'll be able to navigate those scars, literally and figuratively, in the most profound and intentional way. And I'll bet that any future scars you face will impact your sense of self worth less and less along the way. Give it a go. What's there to lose?

THE END...FOR NOW.

Nowadays, my anxiety and worrying about all the things doesn't take over my life. Hell, there are months at a time when I don't feel any anxiety at all. And it's not because I'm special and take a magic pill. It's because I cracked the code on how to flip the switch and chose to put my focus in the right places.

I believe, at the heart of all worry and fear, is a deep desire to fit in, be accepted and be loved. It's back to those two big fears in life I talked about at the very beginning of this book — see how we came full circle?

That's where the real work begins, and why all of these tools are the key to not just holding onto dear life to the sinking ship that is your life, but to building the lifeboat to keep you afloat through the choppy waters.

When we can create a sense of belonging and learn how to love and accept ourselves, without using anything from the outside world as a form of validation, the worries and fears start to fade away. So many people use external pieces of their lives to determine their self worth. The number on the scale. Whether or not their marriage succeeds. Whether or not they get married in the first place. If they have kids. If they have a job that fulfills them. If they make more than six figures a year.

Don't even *try* to tell me you haven't felt unworthy when you didn't achieve one of these shiny pennies. We've all been there, sister. And sure, The Seagull Syndrome desires can be nice and add to your life, but all of those external factors should have no impact whatsoever on whether you are accepted and loved. I use the word "should" with intention here. Normally, I hate that word with every fibre of my being and tell my clients to stop should-ing all over themselves on the fucking regular. But in this case, I stand by using it because it's true.

The shiny pennies in life should have no impact whatsoever on whether you are accepted and loved. Your sense of self worth and fully being accepted and loved begins and ends with you and you alone. No other person, thing, achievement or anything you can think of is going to help you feel accepted and loved. The only person that can do that is YOU.

Let's say the worst case scenarios we talked about way back when actually come true...

You fail the test and flunk out of school.

The version of you that hasn't done the work and cultivated love and acceptance for yourself views this as a major fucking failure. You call yourself worthless, get a job flipping burgers at the local fast food joint and convince yourself that there's no point in trying to do anything more with your life because you aren't capable of it.

The version of you that truly loves and accepts yourself? You mourn the misstep and then you ask, "what's next?" You acknowledge that you didn't apply yourself the way you know you're capable of and you take some time to set up an action plan that will allow you to move forward from a place of intention.

Your marriage ends and you get divorced.

The version of you that hasn't done the work and cultivated love and acceptance for yourself sees this as the end of the world. You shut down and alienate yourself from your family and friends and convince yourself that you'll never meet anyone that will love you again.

The version of you that truly loves and accepts yourself? You acknowledge that you were not able to be your best self in this marriage. You had spent so much time dimming the light within you in order to conform to their standards that you lost yourself in the process. The end of this chapter means a new beginning and one that will allow you to forge a new path for your life, with or without a partner, that feels energizing and in line with your desires.

You lose your home because your business fails.

The version of you that hasn't done the work and cultivated love and acceptance for yourself sees this as the beginning of the end. Your home and your business were the only things in your life that told the world that you had made it. Now what? Everyone is going to look at you as a failure.

The version of you that truly loves and accepts yourself? You mourn the loss for a while and remind yourself that you built it once, you can build it again. So you go to live with your parents for a while until you get your feet on the ground and take the time you need to come up with a new business idea that takes off and financially supports you and your family.

Your husband dies in a plane crash.

The version of you that hasn't done the work and cultivated the love and acceptance for yourself crawls into a deep depressive hole and never gets out. Like, ever.

The version of you that truly loves and accepts yourself? You grieve. A lot. You take the time you need to heal. You go to therapy. You accept help from those around you, and ask for it when you need it, even when it's the last thing you want to do. You do the soul care work you need to do for you, and, when you're ready, open yourself up to love again.

Or maybe, just maybe, you actually do get cancer.

If there's anything I've learned from all of the in-fucking-credible womxn who I've met who have battled cancer (many of whom still are in the throws of chemo and beyond), it's that cancer fucking sucks. There's no way around that. And, to be honest, the fact that we don't have a cure yet after all of the years of work towards it genuinely baffles my not so science based heart. And these womxn? They're also the most badass warriors I've ever met in my life. These womxn have put everything they have into living and watching them not just survive but MF thrive with and after cancer has been such a beautiful reminder that all of us have the capacity to climb whatever mountain is placed in front of us and emerge stronger on the other side. So, while cancer can suck my figurative dick, if I do end up getting diagnosed with cancer in my lifetime, I can and will figure it out and support myself through it. *Hell, this book will be due for a once over read, am I right?!*

The thing that most authors and coaches in the personal development space never want you to actually know is that, **when it comes down to the very heart of it all, you already have everything you need inside of you to fly, you magical creature.** All of these tools I shared? They are tried and true methods that will genuinely help your life suck a little bit less when you're going through the mess. And, you guessed it, they are all rooted in YOU. Your inner knowing. Your deepest desires. YOUR fuck yes life. All you need to navigate the trauma, the mess, the overwhelm and beyond is already in you. You're more powerful than you know, my love. And you were made to move mountains.

So take these tools, my story and all of the stories of those who inspired this book into existence and go out there, take inspired action and live your life on purpose, okay? We're in this crazy whirlwind of a journey called life together. Let's really live it.

ACKNOWLEDGMENTS

Thank you to all of the womxn with BRCA and breast cancer who lent their voice, stories and personal experiences to this book and my life. You are warriors and I am so grateful for your transparency.

Thank you to my husband, Kevan, who not only walked me through this entire experience but laughed at my multiple read throughs of the book and convinced me I am, indeed, funny.

Thank you to Caroline, my editor and best friend. Twenty years of friendship and my life is endlessly better because of having you in it. What would I do without you?

Thank you to Elaine, Khaki, Elaine and Dan for helping bring my vision of the book come to life.

Thank you to Rachel, Leanna, Anna and Laura for lending your words, eyes, ears and energy to this endeavor.

To Dad, thank you for going through this with me.

And Mom, for sticking by my side and being my number one "you go girl" cheerleader. The world needs more parents like you.

To the Breasties and Bright Pink — thank you for creating spaces where I've had the opportunity to meet other womxn just like me, many of whom have become some of my closest friends.

And, as always, thank you to my Live Your F*ck Yes Lifers. My podcast listeners, my amazing clients and all of you for supporting everything that I do. You're the real MVPs and I am endlessly grateful for you.